Praying for Priests: A Mission for the New Evangelization

In this timely work, Kathleen Beckman presents the reader with practical ways to be prayerful supporters of those in Sacred Orders who, like Moses, are in need of the intercession of others to be able to successfully maneuver through the battlefield of the world and spread the message of salvation, available only through Jesus Christ, to a people hungering to hear it. While it is true that all the faithful are called to holiness, deacons, priests, and bishops must, in a particular way, practice virtue in order to fulfill the promises they make on their ordination day.

— **Archbishop J. Augustine Di Noia, O.P.**
Titular Archbishop of Oregon City

Praying for Priests: A Mission for the New Evangelization is an eloquent reflection on the reality of the prayerful support needed by priests and bishops. I especially recommend the Scriptural Rosaries for priests, vocations, and reparation. They combine important contemporary needs with a very powerful and proven prayer to the Mother of God.

— **Most Reverend Kevin W. Vann**
Bishop of Orange, California

Kathleen Beckman's book is a masterful work of spiritual simplicity and richness. Drawing upon the Church's treasury of prayers expressive of our Apostolic Faith, she offers to priests and laity alike the graced opportunity to support, strengthen, and console every priest of the Lord Jesus in his priestly life of sacrificial service. I recommend this book to everyone who takes seriously the clarion call of the New Evangelization. To pray for another's spiritual and temporal well-being is an act of true mercy, and to pray for our priests sets the good example of a lived faith for others. I recommend making this book a part of your day, every day.

— **Most Reverend David D. Kagan**
Bishop of Bismarck, North Dakota

Praying for Priests: A Mission for the New Evangelization reminds everyone that one of the most essential works of the laity to support clergy is to pray for priests. Prayer on behalf of priests was highlighted by the recent official publication of the Congregation for the Clergy, *Eucharistic Adoration for the Sanctification of Priests*. Kathleen wonderfully takes the efforts begun by that publication and her own life and work several steps further, explaining important efforts to make this message better known and more intelligible for contemporary women and the contemporary world. This is a book that will move you and make you redouble your efforts to pray for clergy!

—Msgr. Richard Soseman
Official of the Congregation for the Clergy and author of
Reflections from Rome: Practical Thoughts on Faith and Family

When attacks on the priesthood seem to be intensifying, Kathleen Beckman encourages and equips all the faithful to take up the power of prayer and spiritual fellowship, and in a special way calls upon women in the Church to embrace more deeply Jesus's invitation to become spiritual mothers for His priests. This book is of great value for this important and timely mission.

—Msgr. John R. Cihak, S.T.D.
Official at the Holy See and co-author
of *The Catholic Guide to Depression*

Praying for Priests: A Mission for the New Evangelization is filled with insight, encouragement, and inspiration to lead both priests and laity to a more profound love of God's priceless gift of the priesthood.

—Fr. Peter John Cameron, O.P.
Editor of *Magnificat* and author of
Jesus, Present Before Me: Meditations for Eucharistic Adoration

Kathleen Beckman shows us a way to make the blessings of the priesthood outshine and overpower a myriad of new challenges confronting priests:

an increasingly secularized culture, the new atheism, shadow scandal, and pressures produced by the decline in vocations. As a priest, I am both grateful and indebted to her for the rich graces that will come through this work of prayer.

—**Fr. Robert J. Spitzer, S.J., Ph.D.**
President of the Magis Center of Reason and Faith
and author of *New Proofs for the Existence of God:
Contributions of Contemporary Physics and Philosophy*

The Holy Spirit is really moving in the Church today, inspiring many women to become spiritual mothers for priests. Kathleen Beckman's new book gives a powerful boost to this movement as it offers practical advice and personal testimony that will help countless others to better understand and more fully embrace this beautiful calling.

—**Fr. Michael Gaitley, M.I.C.**
Author of *'You Did It to Me': A Practical Guide to
Mercy in Action* and *33 Days to Morning Glory*

In her work *Praying for Priests: A Mission for the New Evangelization*, Kathleen Beckman manifests the deep love for priests that lies at the heart of her calling in providing this wonderful resource for those experiencing a similar call. This book's focus on praying for the *interior renewal of priests* points to the hidden fountain which is meant to strengthen the hearts of priests as they live their vocation in these challenging times. Kathleen's practical suggestions will invite many to join her in this vital mission.

—**Fr. Richard J. Gabuzda**
Executive Director, The Institute for Priestly Formation

Praying for Priests: A Mission for the New Evangelization manifests Kathleen Beckman's many grace-filled experiences with priests and seminarians. The world is sorely in need of the Lord's gifts mediated through his chosen men. Through the lens of the teachings of the Church, Kathleen demonstrates the importance of sacramental priesthood and priestly ministry. I pray her work touches many hearts!

—**Fr. Abbot Eugene Hayes, O. Praem., J.C.D.**
St. Michael's Norbertine Abbey (Silverado, California)

This work of spiritual edification will benefit those young men who are praying for the grace of a priestly vocation as well as those who have begun their seminary studies and are praying for the grace to persevere. Pastors and all priests should find this book a useful tool to encourage young men to take up the most important vocation in the Church, the one on which hangs the salvation of souls.

—**Fr. Romanus Cessario, O.P.**
Saint John's Seminary (Brighton, Massachusetts)

At the Last Supper, Jesus said, "Strike the shepherd and the flock of sheep will be scattered." His words are being fulfilled today. Prayer is a powerful weapon to counter the spiritual attacks on shepherds and flocks, and is especially needed for suffering priests. I am thrilled that there is now a book like Kathleen Beckman's for people to use as they continue to pray for my brother priests and me. It is essential ammunition for the weapon of prayer.

—**Fr. James Kubicki, S.J.**
National Director of The Apostleship of Prayer and author of
A Heart on Fire: Rediscovering Devotion to the Sacred Heart of Jesus

Praying for Priests: A Mission for the New Evangelization is a tangible expression of the powerful words of St. John Vianney: "The priest continues the work of redemption on earth.... The priesthood is the love of the Heart of Jesus." Kathleen Beckman's inspiring book is a compelling reminder to all Catholics of their sacred responsibility to pray unceasingly for our beloved priests.

—**Mother Judith Zuniga, O.C.D.**
Superior General, Carmelite Sisters
of the Most Sacred Heart of Los Angeles

This book is a treasure! It inspires and teaches us the way of spiritual motherhood through Scripture, the Church's teachings, the saints, and personal testimony. All of us who love the Church recognize how desperately we need the New Evangelization, and the ministerial priesthood is at the front line of the battlefield. Kathleen's book has been inspired by the breath of the Holy Spirit for these times and will help all of us respond in a spirit of love, prayer, and sacrifice which will bring about a new fervor in our own spiritual lives that will radiate out to our beloved priests.

—**Marilyn Quirk**
Foundress of Magnificat, A Ministry to Catholic Women
and recipient of the *Pro Ecclesia et Pontifice* award

Praying for Priests: A Mission for the New Evangelization couldn't have arrived at a better time! At this moment in history, the Church and her priests are under attack and need the powerful protection of prayer more than ever. In my work with women, I have learned that part of our giftedness is a heart for others; I have seen firsthand the fruits that come when women exercise their gift of spiritual maternity through prayer. Thank you, Kathleen, for a thoughtful reflection that instructs, encourages, and inspires.

—**Therese A. Polakovic**
President, Endow (Educating on
the Nature and Dignity of Women)

For the woman who considers herself a daughter of the Church, praying for priests is not an option; rather it is a holy duty, a sacred trust, a divine mandate. Kathleen Beckman provides Catholic women with the means to yoke themselves to the spiritual maternity of the Blessed Virgin Mary, be a conduit of grace in the lives of the men who are *in persona Christi*, and thereby, as Fr. John Hardon, S.J., put it, "carry on Mary's role as Mother of the Church in our time." Congratulations, Kathleen, for providing a work that strikes at the hearts of women to let loose a stream of spiritual maternity that flows into the hearts, souls, and ministries of our priests!

—Johnnette S. Benkovic
Founder and President of Women of Grace® and
Host of *Women of Grace*, seen and heard on
EWTN Television and Radio

Once again, Kathleen Beckman edifies and inspires! In *Praying for Priests*, she shines a beacon of light on the power of intercessory prayer for the interior renewal of priests on the front lines. Unfolding the Blessed Virgin Mary's role as Icon of Spiritual Motherhood, she helps readers discover the beautiful vocation of spiritual motherhood for priests. Would that all Catholics boldly join the Blessed Virgin in lifting up, fortifying, and protecting her beloved priest-sons. Beckman not only sounds this clarion call; she leads the charge!

—Barbara McGuigan
Host of EWTN's *Open Line* and *The Good Fight*

Kathleen Beckman's book is a monumental and timely work for priests and laity! In the wake of recent scandals in the Church, the priesthood is in need of restoration, and prayer is the vital source of healing and renewal. This holy work, especially its Rosary reflections, will soothe the wounds and revitalize the hearts of priests. This book provides impetus to join with Mary's intercession for the sanctification of priests and vocations.

—Dr. Margarett Schlientz
Co-founder and Executive Director of the Pope Leo XIII Institute
and Faculty Member at The Institute for Priestly Formation

⚹

Praying for Priests:
A Mission for the New Evangelization

Praying for Priests:
A Mission for the
New Evangelization

Reflections, Testimonies, and Rosaries

by Kathleen Beckman, L.H.S.

Foreword by Fr. Mitch Pacwa, S.J.

SOPHIA INSTITUTE PRESS
Manchester, New Hampshire

Sophia Institute Press
Box 5284, Manchester, NH 03108
1-800-888-9344

www.SophiaInstitute.com

Sophia Institute Press® is a registered trademark of Sophia Institute.

Library of Congress Cataloging-in-Publication Data
Beckman, Kathleen.
  Praying for priests : a mission for the new evangelization : reflections, testimonies, and rosaries / by Kathleen Beckman, L.H.S. ; foreword by Fr. Mitch Pacwa, S.J.
     pages cm
     ISBN 978-1-62282-211-9 (pbk. : alk. paper) 1. Catholic Church — Prayers and devotions I. Title.
     BX2149.2.B43 2014
     248.3'2 — dc23

                                                                2014009459

First printing

To St. John Paul II and
the priests and seminarians
who enrich my life

✼

Mary, Mother of Priests,
Icon of Spiritual Motherhood, and
Star of the New Evangelization,
pray for us.

Contents

Part 2: Scriptural Rosaries for the Mission

Appendices

$\mathcal{H}$

Foreword

When I entered Quigley Preparatory Seminary in September of 1963, well more than five hundred young men of that incoming class began their training for the priesthood on two campuses, preparing for ordination in 1975. We were expected to study for three hours each day, plus attend daily Mass, pray a daily Rosary, confess weekly, and completely refrain from dating. Vatican II went into its second session that fall; the civil rights movement had been stirred by Dr. Martin Luther King's "I Have a Dream" speech at the Washington Mall, and the first Catholic president was in the White House.

The excitement of working toward the priesthood in a world full of such hope began to unravel with the assassinations of President John F. Kennedy, Martin Luther King Jr., and Senator Robert Kennedy. The Vietnam War, the antiwar protests, race riots, and the sexual and drug revolutions made everything even worse.

The Church was not immune to these cultural crises, either. Sociologically, Catholics became well educated and wealthy as a group; many of them looked beyond their Catholic and ethnic ghettoes so as to join the cultural mainstream. Some Catholic religious leaders interpreted the summons of Pope John XXIII to examine the "signs of the times" as permission to evaluate

Catholic doctrine and practice by the standards set by the culture: the primacy of personal freedom, the need for self-expression, and the dictates of psychological health—which were in fact in great flux as various schools of psychology vied with each other.

Many religious and clergy felt free to leave their state of life because personal freedom was more important than the commitments they had made through their vows. Some of them defined their role in terms of the service or work they did and even placed such a priority on their work that they proclaimed that their work *was* their prayer. As a result, some of them thought that traditional prayer was not necessary, others thought that "imposed" prayer such as the Breviary stifled freedom, and others considered the Rosary old-fashioned and anti-ecumenical. Large numbers of seminarians left their training (only thirty-eight members of my preparatory-school seminary class were ordained), and new vocations dried up, while various experiments with liturgy, retreats, and spiritualities came and went. In addition, the general participation of the laity waned significantly as fewer people felt a need to share in these experiments.

Of course, God never abandoned the Church, and His grace stirred deeply through a variety of renewal movements — Cursillo, Charismatic Renewal, Marriage Encounter, a Marian movement in the 1980s, renewed Eucharistic adoration, and many others—that led to a rediscovery of the Catholic Faith and new insights into the depths of the Church's spiritual treasures. The post-conciliar popes demonstrated that they loved Christ and His people more than they cared for mere theories and theological fads. They communicated an excitement for and deep insight into the Faith. Interestingly, from the first year of Pope John Paul II's papal ministry, the number of new seminarians steadily began to rise.

Foreword

This book draws on the energy of the lay movements that have revivified the Church from the 1960s until the present. It draws deeply from the wisdom and insights of the post-conciliar popes and sets forth a way of integrating them so as to help laity and clergy continue the forward-looking trends of authentic Catholic life and spirituality.

Enter the pages of this book and search out the guidance to help you take your place in the Church's pilgrimage into this new springtime of faith — a time of storms, as accompanies every spring, and a time of growth that often results from the storms.

— Fr. Mitch Pacwa, S.J.

꙳

Acknowledgments

First, I gratefully acknowledge Mauro Cardinal Piacenza, former Prefect of the Congregation for the Clergy, for his personal letter of encouragement for this book and for his charity for priests and vocations as articulated in the Congregation's 2012 booklet, *Eucharistic Adoration for the Sanctification of Priests and Spiritual Maternity.*

Without the steady leadership, encouragement, and prayers of Fr. Stephen Doktorczyk, J.C.L., this work would not have been possible. I am deeply grateful for his spiritual direction and untiring work for the promotion of vocations.

I owe a huge debt of gratitude to my editor (and occasional translator), John Nahrgang, a seminarian of the Diocese of Phoenix. I am sincerely grateful for his expertise, patience, and hard work.

This work is supported by the prayer and encouragement of the founding team of the Foundation of Prayer for Priests: Dr. Cindy Hunt, Dr. Margarett Schlientz, Denise Marie Scalzo, Fr. Stephen Doktorczyk, Fr. Al Baca, Fr. Charlie Cortinovis, Fr. Nick Schneider, Mr. and Mrs. Gabriel Ferrucci, and Msgr. John Esseff.

I am most appreciative of the blessing of Most Reverend Kevin W. Vann, Bishop of the Diocese of Orange, and the contribution of Mother Judith Zuniga, O.C.D., Superior General of the Carmelite Sisters of the Most Sacred Heart of Los Angeles. I gratefully acknowledge the guidance and prayers of Fr. Raymond Skonezny, Fr. Jeff Droessler, and the Norbertine Fathers of St. Michael's Abbey.

To my beloved sisters in Magnificat, A Ministry to Catholic Women; Endow; and Women of Grace, thank you for blessing me as you do. May our respective work of spiritual maternity of priests continue with fresh fervor for the New Evangelization!

Throughout the development of this book, I have relied on the grace of daily Eucharist and the Rosary. I ardently thank Jesus, the Eternal High Priest, and Mary, Mother of Priests, for the many graces that coalesced for this work.

I entrust this book to the Church for the New Evangelization and the glory of the Most Holy Trinity!

Kathleen Beckman, L.H.S.
Orange, California, USA
January 1, 2014
Solemnity of Mary, Mother of God

ॐ

Introduction

I recently came across various works of Pope John Paul I, who reigned as Supreme Pontiff for only thirty-three days in 1978. In one address, the Smiling Pope gave examples of some well-known people who always made sure to have a rosary on their person. His reasons for citing these examples merit reflection:

> The Rosary is contested by some. They say: it is a prayer that is infantile, superstitious and not worthy of a Christian adult. Or else, it is a prayer that is automatic, reduced to a hasty repetition of Ave Marias, monotonous and boring. The crisis of the Rosary was in second place only to the crisis with prayer in general.[1]

The same pontiff invoked Mary at the close of his homily at the Mass to open his pontificate:

> May Our Lady, who guided with delicate tenderness our life as a boy, as a seminarian, as a priest and as a bishop, continue to enlighten and direct our steps, in order that,

[1] Pope John Paul I, quoted in *Magnificat* magazine (October 2013): 110-111.

as Peter's voice and with our eyes and mind fixed on her Son Jesus, we may proclaim in the world with joyous firmness our profession of faith: "You are the Christ, the Son of the living God" (Mt 16:16). Amen.[2]

John Paul I's simple words give us much food for thought. We might ask ourselves what our attitude is toward the holy Rosary. Do we truly believe in the efficacious nature of asking, even begging, Mary to bring our needs to the feet of her Son? Not that the Rosary is the only way we should pray, but Catholics should include it as part of their daily prayer.

The importance of the Blessed Mother in the lives of each of us was echoed by Popes John Paul II and Benedict XVI. Pope Francis recently consecrated the entire world to Mary. These Vicars of Christ realize that without the intercession of the spotless Virgin, our prayer lives would be incomplete.

Nor should anyone shrink from his responsibilities. Laypeople should not underestimate their important role in the Church, which continues to be echoed by Pope Francis. Fifty years ago, at the Second Vatican Council, the Council Fathers stated:

> The sacred pastors know very well how much the laity contribute to the welfare of the whole Church. They know that they themselves were not established by Christ to undertake alone the whole salvific mission of

[2] Pope John Paul I, Homily for Holy Mass for the Inauguration of the Petrine Ministry of the Bishop of Rome, St. Peter's Square, September 3, 1978, http://www.vatican.va/holy_father/john_paul_i/homilies/documents/hf_jp-i_hom_03091978_en.html. Note that the *our* and *we* are more commonly rendered *my* and *I* today.

Introduction

the Church to the world, but that it is their exalted office to be shepherds of the faithful and to recognize the latter's contribution and charisms in such a way that all, in their measure, will with one mind cooperate in the common task.[3]

Two generations have passed since the close of the Council on December 8, 1965. The Church has experienced ups and downs during that time. Most practicing Catholics would not find it difficult to remember positive experiences they and their families have had with priests, often connected with the celebration of a sacrament, visits to the parish school, regular celebration of Sunday Mass, and so forth. Sadly, not everyone's experiences have been positive, and the actions of some priests have had and will continue to have negative consequences for the Church and her members.

What are we to do? Recently, the Congregation for the Clergy rolled out an initiative promoting the sanctification of priests. The Congregation is responsible for, among other things, the "sanctification and effective exercise of [priests'] pastoral ministry."[4] As such, it wishes to involve as many as possible in praying for bishops, priests, and deacons. Experience shows that everyone's involvement in this regard is needed. This initiative is in line with the Church's exhortation that the entire Christian community foster vocations to the priesthood: "This duty especially binds Christian families, educators, and, in a special way, priests, particularly pastors."[5]

---

[3] Vatican Council II, *Lumen Gentium* (Dogmatic Constitution on the Church), no. 30.
[4] John Paul II, Apostolic Constitution *Pastor Bonus*, art. 95 §3.
[5] *Code of Canon Law*, canon 233 §1.

Praying for Priests

Kathleen Beckman, a laywoman devoted to praying both for priests in very specific ways and for vocations to the priesthood, was enthusiastic when she read the first booklet of the Congregation for the Clergy promoting the sanctification of priests in 2007. The same Congregation presented the initiative anew and more substantially in 2012, strongly encouraging individuals and groups to pray for priests' holiness. Kathleen became convinced of the Lord's hand in this initiative. She approached others who expressed their desire to offer their talents in this regard. Kathleen summarized and logically laid out an action plan to help promote the initiative. This was communicated to the then prefect, His Eminence Mauro Cardinal Piacenza, who wrote back indicating his pleasure and support. This book is one of the fruits.

Because Kathleen firmly believes that holier priests will lead to a holier Church, her principal desire is to encourage readers to pray for priests, to offer up sufferings and sacrifices for them, and to pray that families might encourage certain of their members to consider seriously that God might be calling them to the priesthood. The principal prayer is the holy Rosary. Here Kathleen does not reinvent the wheel. Rather, she presents a centuries-old tradition in fresh ways.

As John Paul I stated, there is resistance among some to praying the Rosary. However, I would invite readers to take note that, in this book, with each of the twenty mysteries there is also a specific prayer intention—for priests, for vocations to the priesthood, and for healing, along with reflections from papal documents and an inspired petition to present to the Lord.

Why pray the Rosary? Again, John Paul I stated, "The Rosary, a simple and easy prayer, helps me to be a child and I am not ashamed at all." He also quoted Blessed Charles de Foucald:

Introduction

"Love is expressed with few words, always the same and always repeated."[6]

One might argue that priests should be responsible to pray for themselves. Indeed, seminarians are to be taught the necessity of prayer, the importance of setting aside time each day for mental prayer and other forms of prayer, such as the Liturgy of the Hours and the Rosary. Developing good habits of prayer in the seminary helps one to continue these ways as a priest. To be sure, priests are expected to pray in the above-mentioned ways. The Church earnestly recommends that priests celebrate the Holy Sacrifice of the Mass each day,[7] and we as priests are expected to be faithful to this expectation.

Yet the demands on priests can weigh heavily. Priests rely on the prayers of others. When others pray and offer up some of their sufferings for the Church, for priests, and for vocations to the priesthood, so much good is done. The Lord honors this. It is pleasing to Him. And His Mother, our Mother, indeed wishes to bring to the feet of her Son the intentions we present to her. Kathleen Beckman assists us in this regard by devoting all twenty mysteries of the Rosary to the sanctification of priests.

In addition, five Mysteries of Light are dedicated to praying for vocations to the priesthood. While most parishes in North America are at least able to "get by" with the priests they have, there are other parts of the world where the people rejoice if a priest is able to get to their church once a year. So we should not limit our prayers for vocations only to our backyard but rather extend them to the universal Church. As the author mentions, those who perceive priests in a negative light will usually not

---

[6] Cf. *Magnificat* magazine (October 2013): 111.
[7] *Code of Canon Law*, canon 904.

encourage their sons to consider priesthood. With the help of your prayers, let us hope these perceptions will slowly become more positive and people will better understand the lofty vocation of the priest.

While this inspired book focuses primarily on the sanctification of priests, the author is not unaware that obstacles can prevent people from fully embracing this important initiative. There are those who suffer and are in need of our prayers. Some people have had a bad experience with a priest and remain unsettled. For others, news of the sexual abuse scandal has resulted in their leaving the Church. And with advances in technology, news of a priest who stumbles on the other side of the world is made public worldwide, giving some the impression that no priest can be trusted. Nor can the victims of sexual abuse be overlooked or forgotten; rather, they should be assisted in receiving the healing power of Jesus Christ. Of course, we are all in need of healing, but sometimes there are obstacles in the way. Forgiving others is not always easy. Realizing this, Kathleen Beckman devotes five Sorrowful Mysteries of the Rosary, along with reflections and petitions, to the healing of past and present hurts.

I can attest that the author practices what she preaches. She prays a daily Holy Hour in front of the Blessed Sacrament. Her experiences as a wife and mother have taught her much. Many people have opened up to her with their struggles and difficulties. She generously listens to them and prays for them. She is aware of difficulties facing priests and Catholics in general. Her involvement in healing and deliverance ministry has exposed her to the evil present in the world. All these things she takes to prayer regularly. This is how she was able to formulate the petitions and the particular intentions connected with each mystery of the Rosary.

Introduction

I trust that you will find this book helpful, and I encourage you to be steadfast in your prayer. If this practice has slipped away, please do your best to regain it. If you have never really prayed, let the recitation of the mysteries of the holy Rosary be a healthy starting point. You will find these mysteries more enriching as you progress in your spiritual journey.

Finally, thank you for your interest in priestly holiness and for your desire to contribute to this mission.

—Fr. Stephen Doktorczyk, J.C.L.
Official, Congregation for the Doctrine of the Faith

༄

Praying for Priests:
A Mission for the New Evangelization

Part 1

⁕

The Mission and
the Invitation

1

⚜

Why We *Must* Pray for Priests

When people want to destroy religion they begin by attacking
the priest; for when there is no priest, there is no sacrifice:
and when there is no sacrifice, there is no religion.[8]
—St. John Vianney

In 2009, the Solemnity of the Sacred Heart of Jesus, celebrated on June 19 that year, marked two significant events: the 150th anniversary of the death of St. John Vianney (August 4, 1859), the patron saint of priests, and the start of the Year for Priests. The Year for Priests was declared by Pope Benedict XVI and was intended to "deepen the commitment of all priests to *interior renewal* for the sake of a stronger and more incisive witness to the Gospel in today's world."[9] I was present for the inaugural Mass of the Year for Priests at the National Shrine of the Immaculate Conception in Washington, D.C., celebrated by His

---

[8] Quoted in Abbé Alfred Monnin, *Life of the Curé d'Ars* (Baltimore: Kelly & Piet, 1865), 281.

[9] Pope Benedict XVI, *Inaugural Letter for the Year for Priests*, 2009.

Eminence Theodore Cardinal McCarrick and 130 other priests. It was a glorious liturgy, in which the cardinal elaborated on the gift of ministerial priesthood, the Sacred Heart of Jesus, and the necessity of asking God to renew priests each day. He implored the laity to celebrate the Year for Priests *with* priests and *for* priests so that God might bless them and they might do what God wanted them to do in the year designated *for* priests. He also praised the priesthood of St. John Vianney, who famously described the priesthood as "the love of the heart of Jesus."

The cardinal reminded the priests that no one merits the great gift of God's love, which chose them for priesthood; that from the womb they were called to be transformed into God's love for the Church. He invited priests to thank Jesus for *breaking* His Heart for them. He shared how priests have seen the glory of God in a newly baptized baby, in an old dying nun, in the face of a soldier in battle, in Catholic parents open to life (children), in the prisoner and in the wonder of mercy, in pronouncing the words of the Consecration over bread and wine, when they raise their hand in absolving sins, when a little girl receives her first Holy Communion and whispers, "I love You so much, Jesus." Priests see the glory of divine love in the wonder of the sacrifice of their lives as *alteri Christi* ("other Christs").

That Mass was a perfect precursor to the next day, the feast of the Immaculate Heart of Mary, when, at the same basilica, I had the honor of attending the priestly ordination of a dear friend who became my prayer partner during his years in a seminary in Rome. During his ordination, I perceived the mystical union of this *alter Christus* to his Bride, the Church. By making a total gift of himself to God and His Church, he would discover the embrace of a divine love that would bring him utmost fulfillment and fecundity. It was a great privilege to see the culmination of his many years of formation. The Scripture passage "I am the good shepherd. The good shepherd lays down his life for the sheep" (John 10:11), came to mind during his ordination. I experienced the maternal love of Mary and rejoiced in the making of another priest!

The Importance of the Priest

We desperately need more holy priests to reflect the light of Christ, reveal the tenderness of His Sacred Heart, radiate the beauty of His Holy Face, proclaim the truth of His Word, and extend the power of the seven sacraments. The *Catechism of the Catholic Church* describes sacramental priesthood in this way: "Holy Orders is the sacrament through which the mission entrusted by Christ to his apostles continues to be exercised in the Church until the end of time: thus it is the sacrament of apostolic ministry."[10] And St. John Vianney put it even more succinctly: "Without the Sacrament of Holy Orders we would not have the Lord."[11] Sometimes we do not realize the importance of the priest until we experience the need for God's help. We then look to His minister to aid us. At all times, the priest is vitally necessary to the life of the Church and the salvation of souls.

The Lord has graciously brought many priests and seminarians into my life, beginning with a small group of priests who gathered at our home to pray the Rosary each week during the early to mid-nineties. Since 1992, I have had the honor of serving in the leadership of Magnificat, A Ministry to Catholic Women, an apostolate based on the Visitation (Luke 1:39-51)

---

[10] *Catechism of the Catholic Church* [CCC], no. 1536.

[11] Quoted by Pope Benedict XVI in his Inaugural Letter for the Year of Priests, 2009.

and dedicated throughout eighty international chapters to pro-claiming Mary's *Magnificat* hymn of praise. Through this apos-tolate, I have traveled extensively and crossed paths with many priests. Twelve years ago, a group of priests invited me to join the healing and deliverance team of my diocese. Through these experiences, God and His servants taught me much about the spirituality of ministerial priesthood and, I believe, confirmed me in the charism[12] of intercessory prayer for priests.

In 2004, I published the first of several books dealing with themes such as suffering, the Eucharist, prayer, and the Rosary. I was later invited to attend annual training conferences on healing and deliverance at Mundelein Seminary in Illinois. I met more bishops, priests, and seminarians and eventually was invited to speak at seminaries in both America and Europe. In 2012, the national director of Radio Maria asked me to host a weekly radio program to interview priests, bishops, and lay leaders.

I am now blessed to be the "prayer partner" of a group of priests and seminarians, and it is an undeserved joy to have them in my life. In my travels to seminaries and priest conferences, I have met many heroes, because priests and seminarians are men of brave heart in a world that increasingly rejects the gospel.

I am aware of the challenge that priests face as they strive toward the goal of living like Christ. They acknowledge their individual powerlessness but say yes to God's power working in

---

[12] *Charism* in this sense is defined as "a spiritual gift or talent granted by God to the recipient not primarily for his own sake but for the benefit of others" (*New Catholic Encyclopedia*, s.v. "charism," accessed December 3, 2013, http://www.encyclope-dia.com/article-1G2-3407702279/charism.html).

them. They become burden-bearers for Christ and His people. In presenting themselves for the sacrament of Holy Orders, they step out in faith and into something much greater than themselves. Their good example helps the people of God to do the same.

The science of love taught by Christ consists of sacrificial love for God and neighbor, perfected in missionary zeal. It should only be for love that a priest agrees to follow Jesus in the ministerial priesthood. God help him if it is for any other reason. He is able to make a total gift of himself to Christ because he has experienced a love that is more powerful than anything else.

Here I am reminded of the famous words of Fr. Pedro Arrupe, S.J.:

> Nothing is more practical than finding God, i.e., than falling in love in a quite absolute, final way. What you are in love with, what seizes your imagination will affect everything. It will decide what will get you out of bed in the morning, what you will do with your evenings, how you spend your weekends, what you read, who you know, what breaks your heart, and what amazes you with joy and gratitude. Fall in love, stay in love, and it will decide everything.[13]

Falling in love with Christ creates an inner dynamism of the heart that spurs us selflessly to serve the Beloved. A person in love with God will do amazing things because *nothing* is more

---

[13] Quoted by Fr. James Martin, S.J., *The Jesuit Guide to (Almost) Everything: A Spirituality for Real Life* (New York: HarperCollins, 2010), 219.

dynamic than a love that "bears all things, believes all things, hopes all things, endures all things" (1 Cor. 13:7). Love is like a fire in the soul. It can be a resting flame that, when God gives the word, ignites into a roaring fire that zealously proclaims, "Jesus is Lord!" Love is the essence of Christ's priesthood.

The ordained priest pours himself out as a beloved son of the Father, a chaste spouse of the Church, a spiritual father of souls, a spiritual physician, a head and shepherd within the Church.[14] Pope Benedict XVI reflects upon the notion of priesthood radiating "the love of the heart of Jesus": "The expression of St. John Vianney also makes us think of Christ's pierced Heart and the crown of thorns which surrounds it. I also think, therefore, of the countless situations of suffering endured by many priests, either because they themselves share in the manifold human experience of pain or because they encounter misunderstanding from the very persons to whom they minister."[15]

Here we clearly see that the heart of a priest pulses with love that is sacrificial in nature. Self-renunciation endures only when the human will remains docile in order to ascend to union with God's will. Then one lays down his life for the beloved and allows his heart to be pierced, as was the Lord's. This means the priest must possess a kind of availability of spirit, as Pope Benedict XVI eloquently expresses: "Day after day it is necessary to learn that I do not possess my life for myself. Day by day I must learn to abandon myself; to keep myself available for whatever he, the Lord, needs of me at a given moment, even if other things seem

[14] Cf. *Priestly Formation Faculty Manual* (Omaha: The Institute for Priestly Formation, 2012), 16.
[15] Pope Benedict XVI, *Inaugural Letter for the Year for Priests*, 2009.

more appealing and more important to me: this means giving life, not taking it."[16]

A loving heart is also a sensitive heart. Every vocation requires a heart that sees the needs of others. We learn this through the gift of family. A spiritually sensitive heart perceives Christ's presence in the other. The ordained priest marries the family of the entire Church. That is why Christ gives priests His Sacred Heart with which to love God's family. Ven.[17] Archbishop Fulton Sheen writes about the sensitive disposition of the heart of a true priest:

> Every true priest has the same heart-tearing pity as he flies over a great city such as Paris, New York or London. Down below he sees with Christ's eyes millions of souls unfed by the Eucharist, unhealed by penance, living in houses built on sand because they know not the Rock. He sees in them what Our Lord saw when he looked at the multitudes — danger of eternal loss! Here are countless acres ripe for harvesting, but how few the laborers to gather! Our Lord indicates that this harvest of souls is convertible. He is enthusiastic about the prospects of winning souls, and his words are intended to project that enthusiasm to his priests. He made a similar expression of confident anticipation when the crowds streamed out of Samaria to hear his words, "Why, lift up your eyes, I

---

[16] Pope Benedict XVI, Homily at the Ordination Mass for Fifteen deacons of the Diocese of Rome, in Rome, May 7, 2006.

[17] *Ven.* is the abbreviated form of the title *Venerable*, which is designated to a person declared to be "heroic in virtue" by the Church and signifies a particular stage in the canonization process, which ends in the proclamation of that person as a Catholic saint. This title succeeds Servant of God and precedes Blessed.

tell you, and look at the fields, they are white with the promise of harvest already" (John 4:35).[18]

A loving heart is a vulnerable heart and therefore capable of being wounded, just as the Lord's Sacred Heart was pierced for the salvation of souls. The priest's heart is particularly vulnerable because of his *unique priestly victimhood* with Jesus. For the priest who lives the reality of his human weakness and carries in his heart the pain and suffering of his flock, the cross becomes the right place and perfect provision of God where he can place himself and his people. The priest is above all a victim of divine love; one who has been captured for love. He mysteriously becomes the victim of his own intercession on the cross.

When priests possess hearts that are unwilling to sacrifice and be vulnerable, they can veer off the path that Christ intends for them. Pope Francis provided a warning regarding this in a homily at a Chrism Mass early in his pontificate:

> Those [priests] who do not go out of themselves, instead of being mediators, gradually become intermediaries, managers. We know the difference: the intermediary, the manager, "has already received his reward," and since he doesn't put his own skin and his own heart on the line, he never hears a warm, heartfelt word of thanks. This is precisely the reason for the dissatisfaction of some, who end up sad — sad priests — in some sense becoming collectors of antiques or novelties, instead of being shepherds living with "the odor of the sheep."[19]

[18] Fulton Sheen, *The Priest Is Not His Own* (San Francisco: Ignatius Press, 2005), 80.

[19] Pope Francis, Homily at Chrism Mass, given at St. Peter's Basilica, Rome, March 28, 2013.

The words of Pope Francis are repeated very often and seem to have struck a chord in the hearts of priests and laity alike. They remind us of the communal life of the Church and serve as an important warning against isolation. Sometimes the smell of the sheep is unpleasant, but the Good Shepherd never leaves them. He lays down His life for the flock. He chases after the least of them, and so should priests.

When we see a priest, we behold an ordinary man, but there is much more than meets the eye. A priest elicits certain aspirations within us since most people expect to perceive something of God in him. He also remains a mystery to most people, sometimes even to himself. This should not be cause for concern. The things of God tend to draw us up into beautiful mysteries worth pondering. God's mysteries are not to be solved, but they are embraced in faith. God, the source of all holiness and mystery, desires to remain with us through the person of the priest.

When we perceive holiness, we not only respond with appreciation, but we also desire to have it for ourselves. Peter said, "As obedient children, do not be conformed to the passions of your former ignorance, but as he who called you is holy, be holy yourselves in all your conduct; since it is written, "You shall be holy, for I am holy" (1 Pet. 1:14-16).

Archbishop Sheen expresses well the role of the priest in the sanctification of God's people:

> As the shepherd, so the sheep; as the priest, so the people. Priest-victim leadership begets a holy Church. Every worldly priest hinders the growth of the Church; every saintly priest promotes it. If only all priests realized how their holiness makes the Church holy and how the Church

begins to decline when the level of holiness among priests falls below that of the people![20]

Perhaps, more than we realize, the lay faithful take a cue from a priest's commitment to God. If we perceive authentic fervor, we are inspired. But if fervor seems lacking, we can try to excuse our own mediocrity. Yet it's also true that "holy Christians guarantee holy priests."[21] If we want to be inspired by our priests, we need to be people who inspire them.

Writing to his brother priests about their effect on others, Archbishop Sheen offers more insight: "Every slightest failing on our part brings the community under the judgment of God. Every least increase of priestly virtue brings it blessing."[22] I'd like to relate a story of how the presence of a priest brought God's blessing to a family. Not long ago, a priest friend called and asked me to join him at the hospital and pray for a family in dire need of a miracle. In a hospital room I found the priest and the patient's extended family in a circle of prayer around their loved one, a married man and father of two young sons, who had been diagnosed with a life-threatening disease. Hospital staff had told his wife that she should take him home and try to enjoy the time she had left with him. Unable to accept that prognosis, she called her parish priest, who led us in prayers imploring God's healing upon his parishioner. The priest's ardent supplications reflected his profound confidence in God's healing power. His priestly presence changed the atmosphere in that hospital room. Where a death sentence had been pronounced, this priest was now *pronouncing life* and reminding us that God is the Divine

---

[20] Sheen, *The Priest Is Not His Own*, 76-77.
[21] Ibid., 79.
[22] Ibid., 83.

Physician and Master of Life. God alone would have the final say. The beleaguered family drank in the priest's faith and love as they hung on his words of hope. The priest and my family continued to support him and his family through the highs and lows of different medical treatments for years. His wife championed his cause, always seeking the best. This young father was ultimately given a successful bone-marrow transplant. As a result of brain surgery, he is now legally blind, but he is alive and thriving. His family has also returned to the practice of their faith, filled with gratitude to God for this miracle and for their priest, who helped them carry a heavy cross all the way to resurrection. A priest's availability and fatherly care make all the difference.

If the priest is to remain completely available to God and His people and willing to embrace suffering, *he needs perennial renewal.* St. Gregory of Nazianzus, as a very young priest, had this to say about the interior renewal of the priest:

> We must begin by purifying ourselves before others; we must be instructed to be able to instruct, become light to illuminate, draw close to God to bring him close to others, be sanctified to sanctify, lead by the hand and counsel prudently. I know whose ministers we are, where we find ourselves and to where we strive. I know God's greatness and man's weakness, but also his potential. Who then is the priest? He is the defender of truth, who stands with angels, gives glory with archangels, causes sacrifices to rise to the altar on high, shares Christ's priesthood, refashions creation, restores it in God's image, recreates it for the world on high and, even greater, is divinized and divinizes.[23]

[23] Quoted in CCC, no. 1589.

Interior renewal for a priest who is *with Christ*, the head of the Body, is costly to him. It takes him to a place of extreme humility. Considering that Jesus was born in a manger and died on a cross, the priest learns what St. John Vianney meant when he said, "God has given each of us our own work to do. It for us to pursue our road, that is to say, our vocation.... When God gives us such a vocation, he bestows upon us at the same time his grace to fulfill it."[24] The priest is called to fulfill the mission of carrying the cross, *but God never ordained that he do this alone.*

The Lord requests that *we make sacrifices* in order to bring about a renewal of the priesthood. He wants His flock to have the shepherd close to them, to feed and protect them on the steep path that leads to heaven. God mandates mutual charity because *He makes it possible to love.*

In a beautiful book called *St. Thérèse of Lisieux: Spouse and Victim*, Fr. Cliff Ermatinger explains: "But what God asks of us is not simply to love him with all our heart, but through the dynamic of theological virtue, to love him with *his heart*; that is, with his own divine charity present in our hearts."[25] Even as a little child, Thérèse perceived during a trip to Rome that priests need prayer. Probably because of her spiritual childhood, she could be sensitive to the needs of priests. She later entered religious life with the Carmelites and became one of the famous saints whose lives were offered up as an oblation for priests.

The vocation of all believers to love and serve cannot be "turned off." The divine love first poured into our hearts at baptism is always "on" so that we might be animated to "do whatever

---

[24] Quoted in *Priestly Formation Faculty Manual*, p. 19.

[25] Cliff Ermatinger, *St. Thérèse of Lisieux: Spouse and Victim* (Washington, D.C.: ICS Publications, 2010), 35.

he tells you" (John 2:5). Love is the one thing necessary that compels us to pray and sacrifice for priests, and priests are worthy of receiving the firstfruits of our prayers and sacrifices.

Despite our personal experiences with different priests, we can ask Mary to help us to see them with her eyes, since "for her, a priest is always a priest, a living image of her Son, and if that image is disfigured by sin, she only has a more ardent desire to give him back that resemblance to Christ, for she sees him as God sees him."[26]

The Importance of Praying for Priests and Vocations

The apostle John writes, "And this is the confidence which we have in him, that if we ask anything according to his will he hears us. And if we know that he hears us in whatever we ask, we know that we have obtained the requests made of him" (1 John 5:14-15). Holy Scripture, life experience, and the testimonies of laypeople and clergy have convinced me that prayer is always effective!

The power of prayer should never be underestimated. Christ and His Church have always taught the fundamental importance of communal and personal prayer. St. John Vianney addresses the primacy of prayer:

> Prayer is the source of all graces, the mother of all virtues, the efficacious and universal way by which God wills that we should come to him. He says to us: "Ask, and you shall receive." None but God could make such promises and keep them. He says to us, "If you ask the Father anything in my name, he will give it to you." ... Ought not this

---

[26] Fr. Marie Dominique Philippe, O.P., quoted in *Magnificat Year for Priests Companion* (New York: Magnificat, 2009), 51.

promise [to] fill us with confidence, and to make us pray fervently all the days of our poor life? Within the reach of the ignorant, enjoined to the simple and to the enlightened, prayer is the virtue of all mankind; it is the science of all the faithful! Everyone on earth who has a heart, everyone who has the use of reason ought to love and pray to God.[27]

I have been blessed to cross paths on a few occasions with Fr. Raniero Cantalamessa, O.F.M. Cap., who has served as the Preacher to the Papal Household since 1980, and I am always edified by his joyful presence and his prophetic preaching. He perceives a present movement of the Holy Spirit in the Church that is calling growing numbers of faithful to pray and sacrifice to support the holiness of priests:

> It is true that laypeople contribute to the support of the clergy, but their contribution to the kingdom and to the priests should not stop there. The Lord today is calling the faithful in ever-growing numbers to pray, to offer sacrifices, in order to have holy priests. A concern, a passion, for holy priests has spread as a sign of the times throughout today's Church. Mother Teresa of Calcutta continued to repeat this need. Having heard the cry of the poor in the world, whenever she found herself addressing priests she conveyed that cry (as she did once before the synod of bishops), saying, "They told me to tell you that they need holy priests."
>
> The royal and universal priesthood of believers has found a new way of expressing itself: contributing to the

---

[27] Quoted in *Magnificat Year for Priests Companion*, 28.

sanctification of ministerial priesthood. Such vocations are extending out more and more beyond the walls of the cloistered monasteries, where they have been hidden, and are reaching the faithful. This vocation is becoming widespread, a call that God addresses to many. Through prayer, people are supporting the proclamation of the word and increasing its effectiveness and its fruitfulness. I share with you my time, my study, and the understanding that I acquired from the treasure house of the Church, but others, who are unknown, have contributed the most precious thing: prayer and suffering.[28]

Here, Fr. Cantalamessa clearly acknowledges the hidden offering of prayer and suffering for priests by the laity as a precious gift. And when Mother Teresa refers to the plea of the poor for more holy priests, it reminds us of the dire needs of the poor and their longing to see Christ in a priest who is present to their suffering. The wealthy also possess this longing, for Mother Teresa referred often to the spiritual poverty of wealthy nations. Praying for priests is increasingly important for everyone.

I know many people who have fervent and fruitful prayer lives. But for a greater number of people, the art of prayer is an abandoned one. The Lord is calling His Church to be *first and foremost a house of prayer*. Prayer is paramount to discipleship because prayer connects us with the Sacred Heart of Jesus and His priestly intentions.

Recently I gave a parish mission outside of my diocese. The parish was without a priest, and the temporary solution was to

[28] Raniero Cantalamessa, O.F.M. Cap., *Sober Intoxication of the Spirit, Part Two: Born Again of Water and the Spirit* (Cincinnati: Servant Books, 2012), 60-61.

appoint a lay administrator. The poor parishioners missed their priest very much. Their desolation from not having a pastor was evident. I was edified to discover that a group of women at the parish had begun to pray the Rosary before the tabernacle each week to intercede for the return of a priest to their parish.

We each have a responsibility to work in the vineyard of the Lord and to ask the Lord of the harvest to send more laborers (cf. Matt. 9:38). Pope John Paul II articulates the vital role of the lay faithful in his apostolic exhortation *Christifideles Laici*.[29] I encourage all laypeople seeking a deeper understanding of their role in the universal Church to read this document, which is accessible on the Internet. Historically, the laity have called down showers of grace for the needs of the Church, and recent popes have enthusiastically encouraged the faithful to serve the Lord in this way.

Fr. John Hardon, S.J., compellingly expresses both the urgency and the primacy of praying for priests:

> Having taught priests over 30 years, having lived with priests, and having labored for them, loving them and suffering with them—no words I can use would be too strong to state that the Catholic priesthood needs prayer and sacrifice as never before since Calvary....

[29] An apostolic exhortation is a formal type of communication from the Holy Father that can be addressed to one or more groups and often reinforces a Church teaching. In *Christifideles Laici*, Pope John Paul II lays out a mission for how the laity can live out their baptism and the values of the gospel in communion with the Church in today's world. You can find the document online on the Vatican website: http://www.vatican.va/holy_father/john_paul_ii/apost_exhortations/documents/hf_jp-ii_exh_30121988_christifideles-laici_en.html.

But the pressures are experienced by priests with a violence and a virulence such as no one else but a priest can understand. One saint after another has declared that the devil's principal target on earth is the Catholic priest. Priests need, Lord, how they need, special graces from God. We ask, why pray, then, for priests? We should pray for priests and bishops because this has been the practice of the Church since apostolic times. It's a matter of revealed truth. It is a divine mandate.[30]

Fr. Hardon articulates the reality of the spiritual attacks against the ministerial priesthood and the special graces they need from God. He also reminds us of the divine mandate to pray for clergy. And the Holy Spirit is inspiring new spiritual initiatives, all of which are meant to move the New Evangelization forward with priests on the front lines.

In 2007, then again in 2012, the Congregation for the Clergy made an urgent plea to the universal Church, asking the faithful to engage in Eucharistic intercession[31] for priests and vocations to the priesthood. Acknowledging that the "soul of every apostolate is divine intimacy," the Congregation continues to hope that through this spiritual endeavor of prayer, the faithful will have "a greater awareness of the ontological[32] link between the Eucharist

---

[30] Fr. John Hardon, S.J., "The Value of Prayer and Sacrifice for Priests," The Real Presence Association: Fr. John A. Hardon, S.J., Archives, 1998, accessed November 20, 2013, http://www.therealpresence.org/archives/Prayer/Prayer_014.htm.

[31] Eucharistic intercession means to pray for others in the presence of the Blessed Sacrament, such as during a Holy Hour or adoration.

[32] *Ontological* is a term used in metaphysics concerning the nature and relations of being.

and the Priesthood." Mauro Cardinal Piacenza, then the prefect of the same Congregation, addressed "all those devoted to the Eucharistic Heart of Jesus" when he wrote:

> Throughout her over two thousand year history, the Catholic Church, established by Our Lord as the instrument of salvation for mankind, suffered countless crises precipitated by the weakness of its members. Priests, in particular, face many challenges, striving to do the will of God at every moment of their lives, yet confronted with the countless temptations of modern life. These temptations are best overcome with prayer and penance, their own, and the prayers of others on their behalf. Indeed spiritual writers through history have explained the necessity of prayer for the fruitful ministry of priests.[33]

The cardinal's statement reflects the real condition of a priesthood that requires a continuous commitment of prayer "for the fruitful ministry of priests." The Holy See asks that we pray particularly for the *sanctification* of priests. We depend upon priests for sacramental grace, without which our eternal salvation would be in danger. Priests also depend upon the consistent, ardent prayers of God's people, as expressed by Pope Paul VI in 1965: "The Christian faithful, for their part, should realize their obligations to their priests.... Sharing their cares, they should help their priests by prayer and work insofar as possible so that their priests might more readily overcome difficulties and be able

---

[33] Mauro Cardinal Piacenza, quoted in Congregation for the Clergy, *Eucharistic Adoration for the Sanctification of Priests and Spiritual Maternity* (Fort Collins, CO: Roman Catholic Books, 2013), 8.

to fulfill their duties more fruitfully."[34] Like the Eternal High Priest, every priest needs a Simon of Cyrene to help him carry his cross. It is God's design that we need one another to reach the summit of Calvary and, ultimately, resurrection. The priest can ascend Calvary only with the help of the faithful who support him. This is why we laypeople *must* pray for priests.

Fr. Cantalamessa also highlights a special role that women can play in spiritually assisting priests: "God calls some souls to the even higher task of atoning for priests.... Only men can be priests, but the wisdom of God has kept aside a task for women, an even higher task in a certain sense, which the world does not understand and thus rejects with disdain: that of forming priests and of contributing to raising the quality, not the quantity, of Catholic priesthood."[35] This insight is a crucial theme in this book and is an echo of what Jesus Himself expressed to Ven. María Concepción (Conchita) Cabrera de Armida (1862-1937), a Mexican wife and mother of nine. Jesus's words to Conchita express the complementarity of the common and ministerial priesthood in a mutual act of *agape* love[36]:

There are souls, who through ordination receive a priestly anointing. However, there are ... also priestly souls who do not have the dignity or the ordination of a priest, yet

---

[34] Pope Paul VI, *Presbyterorum Ordinis*, no. 9.

[35] Cantalamessa, *Sober Intoxication of the Spirit, Part Two*, 60.

[36] *Agape* love "expresses selfless care and concern for the well-being of the other. In its Christian context it refers to God's deep and active love for the world, expressed in His desire to save it from the power and consequences of sin and death" (Peter M. J. Stravinskas, ed., *Our Sunday Visitor's Catholic Encyclopedia* [Huntington, IN: Our Sunday Visitor, 1991], 48-49).

have a priestly mission. They offer themselves united to
me … these souls help the Church in a very powerful
spiritual way … You will be the mother of a great number of spiritual children, yet they will cost your heart the
death of a thousand martyrs. Bring yourself as an offering for the priests. Unite your offering with my offering,
to obtain graces for them … I want to come again into
this world … in my priests. I want to renew the world by
revealing myself through the priests. I want to give my
Church a powerful impulse in which I will pour out the
Holy Spirit over my priests like a new Pentecost. The
Church and the world need a new Pentecost, a priestly
Pentecost, an interior Pentecost.[37]

I will entrust to you a different martyrdom; you will
suffer what the priests undertake against me. You will
experience and offer up their infidelity and wretchedness.[38]

Conchita was truly a heroic model of spiritual martyrdom and
love for priests. There are some in the Church, Fr. Cantalamessa
among them, who see her as a very important example of faith
for the renewal of the Church, and the Congregation for the
Clergy itself asserts that "she will be of great importance for the
universal Church."[39] In chapter 2, I will explore the connection
between intercessory prayer and the New Evangelization, which
our recent popes have highlighted.

Spiritual martyrdom of love can be understood in light of
Scripture: "Unless a grain of wheat falls into the earth and dies,

---

[37] Jesus to Conchita, quoted in *Eucharistic Adoration for the Sanctification of Priests and Spiritual Maternity*, 28.
[38] Ibid., 29.
[39] Ibid., 28.

it remains alone; but if it dies, it bears much fruit. He who loves his life loses it, and he who hates his life in this world will keep it for eternal life" (John 12:24-25).

God always desires fruitfulness. Ordinary people are called to sacrificial love that bears fruit. When the soul is aflame with divine love, the sacrifice becomes sweet. Praying for priests is both a *necessary* act of charity and a *duty* of discipleship and should not be relegated to convents and monasteries only. If we *all* take up the mission of praying for the outpouring of the Holy Spirit upon priests, the Spirit will surely grant the Church a new infusion of much-needed love, a new Pentecost, a new springtime of faith.

The Virgin Mary and the saints do much to inspire us to support the priesthood through our prayers (in chapter 3, I will discuss in detail the relationship between Mary and priests, and in chapter 4, I will share inspiring stories of heroines of intercessory prayer for priests).

The faithful are called to pray not only for ordained priests but also for vocations. In front of an audience of priests and deacons in 2006, Pope Benedict XVI highlighted the importance of putting prayer into action and attracting others to our joy in God:

> We stir the heart of God. But our prayer to God does not consist of words alone; the words must lead to action so that from our praying heart a spark of our joy in God and in the Gospel may arise, enkindling in the hearts of others, a readiness to say "yes". As people of prayer, filled with his light, we reach out to others and bring them into our prayer and in the presence of God, who will not fail to do his part. In this sense we must continue to pray the Lord

of the harvest, to stir his heart, and together with God touch the hearts of others through our prayer.[40]

Archbishop Sheen points to the *only* specific request that Jesus made about stimulating vocations:

> There is no priest who does not go through the motions of urging the faithful to pray for vocations. But, too often, the phrases are formal. They are what is expected of one. In the priest's mind, they are part of the announcements, on a level with the card party for the Ladies' Auxiliary or the Catholic Youth Organization skating meet.
>
> These other activities are, of course, not to be sneered at. They too foster a Christian life and therefore stimulate vocations. But can we put them in the same category as prayer? Out of hundreds of possible ways of fostering vocations, *prayer* was the *single* one Our Lord specified.[41]

I know several young priests who are assigned to two or more parishes, and this is, of course, hard on everyone. Many parishes rely on priests from other parishes to serve them. Laypeople are not happy in these situations, and many complain about not having a priest available. That makes it all the more urgent and necessary to enlist *all the faithful* in the work of interceding for vocations to the priesthood. We are grateful for the good work of apostolates such as the Serra Club and the many religious communities who intercede for priests daily, but *all the lay faithful* should petition God for holy priests and vocations — not occasionally, but *always*. St. John Vianney reminded his parishioners

---

[40] Pope Benedict XVI, meeting with priests and deacons of Bavaria, Freising, Germany, September 14, 2006.

[41] Sheen, *The Priest Is Not His Own*, 79, emphasis added.

that the priest is not a priest for himself; he is priest for the people of God—for you and me!

The Congregation for the Clergy's initiative and other Church documents invite intercession for priests through family prayer in the home, the formation of prayer groups within parishes or homes, and individual prayer. Every person can respond according to his or her situation. The key is to *engage in the mission of praying*.

Two powerful methods of interceding for priests that are highly recommended by the Congregation for the Clergy include offering a Holy Hour and praying the Rosary. I devote chapter 5 to the splendors of encountering Jesus in the Holy Hour and chapter 6 to the power and beauty of the Rosary, as well as its connection not only to intercessory prayer and priests but also to the Eucharist.

The priest's responsibility is awesome, and he is held to a higher standard that requires a continuous offering of prayer, from him and others. Praying for our beloved priests assumes a deep appreciation for the grandeur of the priestly office and a magnanimous response to Jesus, who exhorts us to ask the Lord to send laborers into His harvest (cf. Matt. 9:38).

Inspiration at Calvary

When some priest friends invited me to join them for a private retreat in the Holy Land in early 2013, I did not hesitate to accept. The Holy Land had become very meaningful to me ever since I had been invested into the Equestrian Order of the Knights and Ladies of the Holy Sepulchre of Jerusalem.[42]

---

[42] This papal order is the only lay institution of the Vatican State charged with the task of providing for the needs of the Latin Patriarchate of Jerusalem and for "all the initiatives which are

Praying for Priests

There is nothing in the world that compares to experiencing the living Gospel in the Holy Land. Its spiritual effect abides in the human heart and brings the Scriptures to life. On the airplane to the Holy Land, I recorded these petitions:

1. The grace to be forgetful of self

2. The grace never to refuse Jesus anything so as always to console His Sacred Heart

3. The grace to be like Mary in all things

On January 31, we visited the Church of the Holy Sepulchre and made a point of praying as long as possible at the Rock of Calvary. I prayed fervently for the sanctification of my family, all priests, and everyone who had asked me to leave their prayer petitions at Calvary. It was not crowded inside, so I was able to rest my head on the Rock of Calvary for a long time and contemplate the perfect sacrifice of my Savior. My heart overflowed with unspeakable gratitude, and I ardently recommitted my life to the Lord through an act of oblation. How could I do otherwise in the place where Jesus had spilled His Precious Blood and covered me in the crimson cloak of redemption?

Later that evening, during private adoration of the Blessed Sacrament in the Garden of Gethsemane, the monstrance was placed on an altar in front of an exquisite mosaic depicting the scene in the garden where Judas betrayed Jesus with a kiss. I was reminded of Judas's kiss of betrayal and how priests share closely in the Lord's agony, and I recalled today's rampant forms of infidelity that wound the Sacred Heart and also the human heart.

---

necessary to support the Christian presence in the Holy Land" (http://www.holysepulchre.net/history/structure.html).

Why We *Must* Pray for Priests

On the feast of the Presentation of the Lord, a small group of us was permitted to remain inside the Church of the Holy Sepulchre after all the visitors had left and the doors had been locked. It was a very chilly, rainy night; even inside the church, it was extremely cold. I sat as close as possible to the Rock of Calvary and prayed in reparation for my sins and for those of the whole world.

I asked Jesus, "If I had been present at the Crucifixion, would I have run away like the other disciples, or would I have stayed with You and Mary and St. John?" He left that inquiry hanging. I prayed, "Lord, I have crucified You through so many small and big infidelities. Please have mercy on me, a sinner."

Then the Holy Spirit reminded me that my spiritual director had just given me the new and expanded edition of *Eucharistic Adoration for the Sanctification of Priests and Spiritual Maternity.* I pondered the contents of the Congregation's booklet and prayed fervently that the Holy See's program would ignite a widespread fervor of prayer for holy priests and more vocations.

I was reminded of the Eternal High Priest, who tenderly engaged Simon Peter: "'Simon, son of John, do you love me?' Peter … said to him, 'Lord, you know everything; you know that I love you.' Jesus said to him, 'Feed my sheep'" (John 21:17). I considered the love of Jesus for Peter and for all priests in the continuous apostolic line. I rejoiced in the intimacy of the unique love that binds the priest to Jesus. I also reflected on the sheep that need the food that only the priest can give—the Eucharist. My hunger for the Bread of Heaven increased, and my soul gave thanks to the Lord for His perfect sacrifice on Golgotha.

After praying for an extended time near the Rock of Calvary, I moved to the right to pray in front of an icon of the Sorrowful Mother with a sword piercing her heart. I pondered and wept.

Mary experienced perfect sorrow at the Crucifixion of her Son. Her heart was pierced so that our thoughts would be laid bare before God and His divine thought could be received into our hearts (cf. Luke 2:35).

In prayer before the icon of Mary's pierced maternal heart, I offered to console the Sorrowful Mother all the days of my life to the best of my ability, with the help of God's grace. In that noble atmosphere at Calvary, during hours of prayer, Mary impressed upon me her maternal intention to pray for priests because there is so much that she wants to do for God's people through her priest-sons. This is what I recorded in my prayer journal then:

> There are priests who have long ago ceased to pray, and even ceased to believe. They are like dry bones withering in the desert heat. They go through the motions bereft of love. Other priests console God because their hearts are pure, their intentions are good, and they persevere to do the will of the Father for love of Jesus. Continue to pray for the conversion of sinners and for the sanctification of the shepherds. Upon the priests rests a heavy weight that must be supported by the increasing prayers of the faithful.

Over the remainder of our two weeks in Jerusalem, I prayed and conferred with my priest companions at the holy sites where Jesus had walked. We asked the Lord to show us if there was a way we might further the Congregation for the Clergy's initiative for the sanctification of priests. We each felt called to do what we could.

After returning home, I consulted with several priest counselors. With their encouragement, I wrote a letter to the prefect of the Congregation for the Clergy outlining a proposal for a media campaign, a book, and, most importantly, an ecclesial movement that would help spread its initiative of prayer for priests, vocations, and spiritual maternity. On May 31, 2013, I received a letter from Mauro Cardinal Piacenza, then prefect, graciously thanking me for the proposal letter and encouraging me to advise my bishop and move forward. I did so, and on September 13, 2013, I received a letter from my bishop, lending his support for the book and for a new apostolate, the Foundation of Prayer for Priests.

Its mission statement declares:

> With explicit support from the Holy See, the **Foundation of Prayer for Priests** is a Eucharistic and Marian apostolate of intercessory prayer and catechesis aimed at obtaining graces for the sanctification of priests and fostering vocations to the priesthood. Affirming the indispensability of priests standing at the forefront of the Church and following the example of the Blessed Virgin Mary, Icon of Spiritual Motherhood,[43] we invite all Catholics to join us in this global mission of prayer and sacrifice for the New Evangelization.

This is not the work of one individual but of an approved team of priests and laity working in conjunction with an ecclesial advisory group to make as fruitful as possible the Holy See's initiative for priests. Through this new apostolate, we hope to unite laity, religious, clergy, and seminarians throughout the Church

[43] I intend *icon* here to mean an image or model that is worthy of emulation. In the Catholic and Orthodox traditions, the icon can be considered a sacred object that provides a means of veneration. This is very meaningful to me, given my profound experience while praying before the icon of Mary at the Church of the Holy Sepulchre.

in a great crusade of intercessory prayer for priests. Appendix 3 of this book has more information on the apostolate and its objectives and explains how to join your prayers and sacrifices for priests with those of many other Catholics around the world.

The priests who are in the sanctuary are vulnerable without a vestment of prayer woven for them by the faithful. May the following words of Jesus to Ven. Conchita stir us all to action and open our hearts to the workings of divine grace!

The Holy Spirit is He who blows, and moves hearts, and lifts them from the earth, and carries them to celestial horizons, and communicates to them the thirst for the glory of God. He is the one who will give them His light and His fire for inflaming the entire earth. Thus I want priests, possessed of the Holy Spirit and forgetful of themselves, all for God, all for souls.

Let them ask for this reaction, this new Pentecost, for my Church needs holy priests through the Holy Spirit.

The world collapses, because faithful priests are lacking who would draw it out of the abyss in which it finds itself; priests of light who would illuminate the paths of goodness; pure priests who would rescue so many hearts from the mire; priests on fire who would fill up the whole universe with divine love.

Ask, cry out to heaven, offer the Word so that all things may be restored in me, through the Holy Spirit, and through Mary.[44]

---

[44] Quoted in Concepción Cabrera de Armida, *A Mis Sacerdotes* (Mexico City: Editorial La Cruz, 1997), 95 (text translated by John Nahrgang).

2

✳

Intercessory Prayer and
the New Evangelization

One form of prayer moves us particularly
to take up the task of evangelization
and to seek the good of others:
it is the prayer of intercession.[45]

—Pope Francis

In the spring of 2010, I traveled to the island of Malta with a priest friend in response to an invitation to speak at a Magnificat event and pray with groups of laypeople, priests, and seminarians. While there, I learned that a young generation of Maltese was working to enact civil laws that for the first time would permit divorce and abortion. At the seminary, local priests anxiously asked for many prayers.

The following spring, I traveled to Poland to speak at a faith conference and a Magnificat prayer breakfast. I learned about a rise in cohabitation among younger generations and more laws

---

[45] *Evangelii Gaudium*, no. 281

permitting abortion. I spoke with Polish priests who expressed a variety of concerns for the Church in Poland.

A few months later, Fr. Kevin Scallon, C.M., and Sr. Briege McKenna, O.S.C., two wonderful people dedicated to ministering to priests all over the world, invited me to speak at an "Intercession for Priests" retreat held at All Hollows College Seminary in Dublin, Ireland. Gazing upon the lush green landscape from the airplane window as we descended over Dublin, I pondered the rich history of both the Church in Ireland and the memory of the many Irish priests and nuns who once populated our American Catholic schools and parishes. But during the entire week of the retreat, my heart became burdened by the condition of the Church in Ireland. Over the weekend, I attended Mass away from the retreat center at a nearby parish church. I experienced an atmosphere of listlessness, sadness, and even spiritual oppression. During the liturgy, there were times when the poor pastor sounded timid and even apologetic!

In these countries, which have an illustrious history of fidelity to the Faith, I met many Catholics who were filled with zeal for God and His Church and were committed to passing down the Catholic Faith to their children and grandchildren. I was touched by laypeople and priests and their perseverance to serve the Church. They came to the retreats in need of restoration and left filled with renewed strength. But my heart was burdened by the apparent condition of the Church in these countries and the path they seemed to be on. They appeared to be slowly losing their Catholic identity, and I could perceive the rising influence of secularism and worldly pressures.

I have had similar experiences speaking in dioceses across the United States. These experiences have opened my eyes to why the New Evangelization is so necessary for the universal Church.

Intercessory Prayer and the New Evangelization

The term *New Evangelization* has now appeared several times in this book and merits an explanation. Pope John Paul II, in his 1990 encyclical[46] *Redemptoris Missio*, notes how the term *evangelization* is typically applied to "peoples, groups, and socio-cultural contexts in which Christ and his Gospel are not known." This is commonly referred to in the Church as the *"missio ad gentes"*[47] (Latin for "mission to the nations"). John Paul II then points out that a "new evangelization" or "re-evangelization" is needed for "entire groups of the baptized [who] have lost a living sense of the faith, or even no longer consider themselves members of the Church, and live a life far removed from Christ and his Gospel."[48]

Two years later, in 1992, Pope John Paul II penned *Pastores Dabo Vobis* (*I Will Give You Shepherds*), an apostolic exhortation that was addressed to bishops, clergy, and all the faithful. It provides key insights into the priestly character formed through the sacrament of Holy Orders and the importance of fruitful cooperation from all the people of God in supporting priests and vocations, especially through intercessory prayer. In it, the Holy Father connected the serious undertaking of priestly formation with the evangelization of souls:

---

[46] An encyclical is another formal type of papal communication that addresses a matter of importance for the whole Church. It is considered to be a kind of teaching document.

[47] This phrase came into use within the Church after the promulgation of *Ad Gentes*, the Decree on the Missionary Activity of the Church, by Pope Paul VI at the Second Vatican Council in 1965. Evangelization was also the core theme of Paul VI's 1975 apostolic exhortation *Evangelii Nuntiandi* (*Evangelization in the Modern World*).

[48] Pope John Paul II, *Redemptoris Missio*, no. 33.

Praying for Priests

The formation of future priests, both diocesan and religious, and the lifelong assiduous care for the personal sanctification in the ministry and for the constant updating of their pastoral commitment is considered by the Church one of the most demanding and important tasks for the future of the evangelization of humanity.[49]

The pope also noted the evolving needs of priests and laity in a world that has drastically changed and requires "new fervor" and "new expression for the announcing and witnessing of the Gospel":

Today, in particular, the pressing pastoral task of the new evangelization calls for the involvement of the entire People of God, and requires a new fervor, new methods and a new expression for the announcing and witnessing of the Gospel. This task demands priests who are deeply and fully immersed in the mystery of Christ and capable of embodying a new style of pastoral life, marked by a profound communion with the pope, the bishops and other priests, and a fruitful cooperation with the lay faithful, always respecting and fostering the different roles, charisms and ministries present within the ecclesial community.[50]

Yes, something new must occur, because I have often prayed with priests who are so overwhelmed by the tasks of evangelization that they are almost paralyzed. The challenges of the present time in the history of the Church can become so demanding on a priest that his heart simply ceases to engage. The laity, by prayer, can help to "jump-start" the priest's heart!

[49] Pope John Paul II, *Pastores Dabo Vobis*, no. 2.
[50] Ibid., no. 38.

Intercessory Prayer and the New Evangelization

The prayers in chapters 7 through 9 and appendix 1 of this book are designed to do exactly that. Prompted by the Holy Spirit, I have composed scriptural Rosaries of intercession that draw from Scripture, *Pastores Dabo Vobis*, and *Salvifici Dolores*, an important apostolic letter also written by Pope John Paul II. These Rosaries are organized according to three prayer intentions: intercession for priests, intercession for vocations, and reparation for the abuse scandal.

In 2003, Pope John Paul II wrote an encyclical entitled *Ecclesia de Eucharistia* (*On the Eucharist in Its Relationship to the Church*), which emphasizes the need to "rekindle Eucharistic amazement" for the "enthusiasm of the new evangelization." This letter is a blueprint for forming contemplatives in action, and this is precisely what is called for in our day:

> I would like to rekindle this Eucharistic "amazement." ... *To contemplate the face of Christ, and to contemplate it with Mary, is the "program" which I have set before the Church at the dawn of the third millennium, summoning her to put out into the deep on the sea of history with the enthusiasm of the new evangelization.* To contemplate Christ involves being able to recognize him wherever he manifests himself, in his many forms of presence, but above all in the living sacrament of his body and his blood. The Church draws her life from Christ in the Eucharist; by him she is fed and by him she is enlightened.[51]

Rekindling Eucharistic amazement is at the core of the New Evangelization. It is the "program" by which we will recover our joy for evangelization. Any lack of Eucharistic amazement and joy

---

[51] *Ecclesia de Eucharistia*, no. 5, emphasis added.

contributes to people leaving the Church, especially the young. Rekindling Eucharistic amazement has been a dominant theme of my weekly Catholic radio program since it began, and I have found the subject to be inexhaustible. Living a Eucharistic life always produces the joy that draws others to Christ and His Church.

Momentum continued to build when, in 2007, as I mentioned before, the Congregation for the Clergy issued its booklet *Eucharistic Adoration for the Sanctification of Priests and Spiritual Maternity*, seeking to ignite a crusade of intercessory prayer for priests and vocations for the "authentic renewal of priestly life":

> In today's world a great many things are necessary for the good of the Clergy and the fruitfulness of pastoral ministry. With a firm determination to face such challenges without disregarding the difficulties and struggles, and with an awareness that action follows being and that the soul of every apostolate is Divine intimacy, it is our intention for the departure point to be a spiritual endeavor: a movement of prayer, placing continuous Eucharistic adoration at the center.[52]

Eucharistic adoration for the sake of priests is the greatest service we can offer for the salvation of souls. It is a key that unlocks the floodgates of divine mercy.

In June 2010, Pope Benedict XVI created the Pontifical Council for Promoting the New Evangelization, expressing the Church's dedication to furthering Pope John Paul II's vision, including: "to make known and to support initiatives linked to the new evangelization that are already being put into practice

---

[52] *Eucharistic Adoration for the Sanctification of Priests and Spiritual Maternity* (2007 edition), 1.

in various particular Churches, and to promote the realization of new projects by actively involving the resources present in Institutes of Consecrated Life and in Societies of Apostolic Life, *as well as in groups of the faithful and in new communities.*"[53] Pope Benedict spoke to the need for new apostolates to effect the New Evangelization. The Holy Spirit will inspire such new communities for the Church *in this hour.*

A few months later, in September of 2010, Pope Benedict XVI wrote the apostolic exhortation *Verbum Domini* and again demonstrated his continuity of thought with his predecessor Pope John Paul II in regard to the New Evangelization:

> Our own time, then, must be increasingly marked by new hearing of God's word and a new evangelization. Recovering the centrality of the divine word in the Christian life leads us to appreciate anew the deepest meaning of the forceful appeal of Pope John Paul II: to pursue the mission *ad gentes* and vigorously to embark upon the new evangelization, especially in those nations where the Gospel has been forgotten or meets with indifference as a result of widespread secularism.[54]

With rising secularism in most countries, there is now an urgent global need to rediscover the gospel message. In October of 2012, Pope Benedict XVI convened a synod of bishops on the topic of "The New Evangelization for the Transmission of the Christian Faith," and again intercession and evangelization were highlighted. Note here the similarity in papal thought for the good of the universal Church:

---

[53] Pope Benedict XVI, *Ubicumque et Semper*, art. 3, emphasis added.

[54] Pope Benedict XVI, *Verbum Domini*, no. 122.

Dear brothers and sisters, let us entrust the work of the Synod meeting to God, sustained by the communion of saints, invoking in particular the intercession of great evangelizers, among whom, with much affection, we ought to number Blessed Pope John Paul II, whose long pontificate was an example of the new evangelization. Let us place ourselves under the protection of the Blessed Virgin Mary, Star of the New Evangelization. With her let us invoke a new outpouring of the Holy Spirit, that from on high he may illumine the Synodal Assembly and make it fruitful for the Church's journey today, in our time. Amen.[55]

Pope Benedict suggests that Pope John Paul II is the embodiment of the New Evangelization! Since Mary is the Star of the New Evangelization, Pope John Paul II, whose papal motto was *Totus tuus*, or "[Mary, I am] totally yours," would naturally be another icon of the New Evangelization.

At the closing of the synod, the bishops emphasized the centrality of contemplating the Eucharist and the Holy Spirit as the *principal agent of evangelization*:

The Eucharist must be the source and summit of the New Evangelization. The Synod Fathers urge all Christ's faithful to renew their understanding and love for the Eucharistic celebration, in which their lives are transformed and joined to Christ's offering of his own life to the glory of God the Father for the salvation of the whole world.

---

[55] Pope Benedict XVI, Homily at the Opening Mass of the Synod of Bishops and Proclamation of St. John of Ávila and St. Hildegard of Bingen as Doctors of the Church, Rome, October 7, 2012.

Intercessory Prayer and the New Evangelization

The principal agent of evangelization is the Holy Spirit, who opens hearts and converts them to God. The experience of encountering the Lord Jesus, made possible by the Spirit, which introduces one into the Trinitarian life, welcomed in a spirit of adoration, supplication and of praise, must be fundamental to every aspect of the New Evangelization. This is the "contemplative dimension" of the New Evangelization which is nourished continually through prayer, beginning with the liturgy, especially the Eucharist, source and summit of the life of the Church.[56]

Here the bishops remind us to allow ourselves to be fed by the Bread of Life and carried on the breath of the Holy Spirit, who leads us forward toward the goal of setting the world ablaze with the love of Christ.

The final closing message of the synod also turned to Mary, Star of the New Evangelization, reminding us to entrust ourselves to her:

The figure of Mary guides us on our way. Our journey, as Pope Benedict XVI told us, can seem like a path across the desert; we know that we must take it, bringing with us what is essential: the gift of the Spirit, the company of Jesus, the truth of his word, the Eucharistic bread which nourishes us, the fellowship of ecclesial communion, the impetus of charity. It is the water of the well that makes the desert bloom. As stars shine more brightly at night in the desert, so the light of Mary, the Star of the new

---

[56] XIII Ordinary General Assembly of the Synod of Bishops, Final List of propositions, October 7-28, 2012.

evangelization, brightly shines in heaven on our way. To her we confidently entrust ourselves.[57]

It is fitting that Mary and the Holy Spirit, the two agents who incarnated Jesus into the world, are the two necessary agents of the New Evangelization. Just a few weeks after the synod ended, the Congregation for the Clergy reissued its booklet strengthening the call for Eucharistic adoration for the sanctification of priests and spiritual maternity, this time adding a protocol for a Eucharistic Holy Hour for priests and inviting the recitation of the holy Rosary and the Chaplet of the Divine Mercy.[58] This invitation by the Holy See is now an essential aspect of the New Evangelization.

And our current Holy Father? It turns out that Pope Francis's vision for the New Evangelization has proven to be an organic progression of his predecessors. This is evident in the November 2013 publication of his apostolic exhortation *Evangelii Gaudium* (*The Joy of the Gospel*), in which the Holy Father uses the word *evangelization* 110 times and the phrase *new evangelization* 14 times! I would like to highlight four themes from this beautiful document.

First, Pope Francis speaks about the Holy Spirit and Mary as central to the New Evangelization and refers to the first Pentecost. For the reasons he describes here, Mary is often invoked and honored as the Star of the New Evangelization: "With the

[57] XIII Ordinary General Assembly of the Synod of Bishops, Final Message, Rome, October 26, 2012.

[58] The Chaplet of the Divine Mercy is a devotion associated with the visions and writings of St. Maria Faustina Kowalska (1905-1938), a Polish nun and victim-soul. More information on the devotion and the chaplet can be found in the Congregation's 2012 booklet or at http://www.thedivinemercy.org/message/devotions/chaplet.php.

Holy Spirit, Mary is always present in the midst of the people. She joined the disciples in praying for the coming of the Holy Spirit (Acts 1:14) and thus made possible the missionary outburst which took place at Pentecost. She is the Mother of the Church which evangelizes, and without her we could never truly understand the spirit of the new evangelization."[59]

Second, Pope Francis references St. Paul in brilliantly connecting intercessory prayer with contemplation:

> One form of prayer moves us particularly to take up the task of evangelization and to seek the good of others: it is the prayer of intercession. Let us peer for a moment into the heart of St. Paul, to see what his prayer was like. It was full of people: "I constantly pray with you in every one of my prayers for all of you ... because I hold you in my heart" (Phil. 1:4, 7). Here we see that intercessory prayer does not divert us from true contemplation, since authentic contemplation always has a place for others.[60]

Third, Pope Francis speaks of the magnanimity of God's people as intercessors and how they touch the heart of God the Father:

> The great men and women of God were great intercessors. Intercession is like "a leaven in the heart of the Trinity." It is a way of penetrating the Father's heart and discovering new dimensions which can shed light on concrete situations and change them. We can trust that God's heart is touched by our intercession, yet in reality he is always there first. What our intercession achieves is that this

---

[59] *Evangelii Gaudium*, no. 284.
[60] Ibid., no. 281.

power, his love and his faithfulness are shown ever more clearly in the midst of the people.[61]

Finally, Pope Francis challenges us all to be at the service of Divine Love so that *our joy may draw others* to God and the Church:

> The Gospel offers us the chance to live life on a higher plane, but with no less intensity: "Life grows by being given away, and it weakens in isolation and comfort. Indeed, those who enjoy life most are those who leave security on the shore and become excited by the mission of communicating life to others." When the Church summons Christians to take up the task of evangelization, she is simply pointing to the source of authentic personal fulfillment. For "here we discover a profound law of reality: that life is attained and matures in the measure that it is offered up in order to give life to others. This is certainly what mission means." Consequently, an evangelizer must never look like someone who has just come back from a funeral! Let us recover and deepen our enthusiasm, that "delightful and comforting joy of evangelizing, even when it is in tears that we must sow. And may the world of our time, which is searching, sometimes with anguish, sometimes with hope, be enabled to receive the good news not from evangelizers who are dejected, discouraged, impatient, or anxious, but from ministers of the Gospel whose lives glow with fervor, who have first received the joy of Christ."[62]

---

[61] *Evangelii Gaudium*, no. 283.
[62] Ibid., no. 10.

Intercessory Prayer and the New Evangelization

When Pope Francis encourages us to "leave security on the shore" for the sake of the New Evangelization, we are reminded of the exhortation of St. Paul, who wrote to the Corinthians about the apostles' becoming fools for Christ: "For I think that God has exhibited us apostles as last of all, like men sentenced to death; because we have become a spectacle to the world, to angels and to men. We are fools for Christ's sake" (1 Cor. 4:9-10). Paul also reminded the Corinthians, "The cross is folly to those who are perishing, but to us who are being saved it is the power of God" (1 Cor. 1:18). God's love is the cause of our joy. Christ's Vicar reminds us that authentic evangelization springs from the joy in a person who has fallen in love with Jesus and has made the gospel the manual of life. Remember, "the joy of the Lord is your strength" (Neh. 8:10).

The previous quotations indicate the continuity of papal and episcopal thought on the themes of: 1) encountering Jesus, 2) the New Evangelization, 3) intercessory prayer, 4) contemplation of the Eucharist, 5) testimony, 6) accompanying the poor, 7) joy, 8) the work of the Holy Spirit for a New Pentecost, 9) entrustment to Mary. And all of these coalesce for the particular, urgent needs of the Church *in her present hour*. In subsequent chapters these themes will be amplified.

Prior to all of these recent movements of the Spirit, Jesus Himself spoke to Ven. Conchita in the early twentieth century about the way the Church will be set ablaze again as by a New Pentecost through the renewal of priests:

A new redemption will come, not by my human passion, but by my passion in crucified souls and a new Pentecost by the living and ardent impulse of the Holy Spirit.... But to save souls, to set souls on fire, to bring souls to perfection, we have to begin by the root, which is the Church in my priests, as a powerful help for the saving work that is going to come, which is at the gates.... I will suffer in souls. I will expiate in souls, I will purchase with my merits — in souls — the new era of fervor in my Church.[63]

Jesus identifies *the Church in priests* as "the root" from which will come a powerful help in the cause of the salvation of souls, in union with the Holy Spirit and other courageous souls. And, as Jesus boldly declares, we have arrived at the point of becoming His instruments in this great and noble undertaking:

The time has come to urge forward the kingdom of the Holy Spirit and to put an impregnable barrier against Satan, spiritualizing souls. But for this reason I have to avail myself of instruments who more intimately belong to Me — My Priests — who are designated for saving the world: but transformed into Me through the Holy Spirit."[64]

Let us take this step forward in faith! Let us pray:

Holy Spirit, in union with Your spouse Mary, Mother of Priests, graciously descend upon humanity in a New Pentecost, sending forth flames of renewal upon the souls of priests and laity. Spread Your Light and Your Love in the New Evangelization to advance the Kingdom of God on earth. Amen.

---

[63] Concepción Cabrera de Armida, *To My Priests: A Translation of A Mis Sacerdotes* (Cleveland: Archangel Crusade of Love, 1996), 48.
[64] *To My Priests*, 119.

3

⚜

Mary, Priests, and Spiritual Motherhood

God the Son wishes to form himself,
and, in a manner of speaking,
become incarnate every day in His
members through His dear Mother.[65]
—St. Louis Marie de Montfort

Mary, Mother of Priests, and the holy Rosary are two pillars of this book, which contains scriptural Rosaries dedicated to priests, vocations, and reparation. Mary's maternal love is the golden thread that ties these together. In Mary we find the icon of spiritual motherhood. As the Mother of God, Mary's "divine maternity" makes her God's sublime gift to the Church, as expressed beautifully by Fr. Reginald Garrigou-Lagrange:

> There can be no question of calling her a priest in the strict sense of the word since she has not received the

---

[65] Quoted in *God Alone: The Collected Writings of St. Louis Marie de Montfort* (Bayshore, NY: Montfort Publications, 1987), 298.

priestly character and cannot offer Holy Mass nor give sacramental absolution. *But . . . her divine maternity is a greater dignity than the priesthood of the ordained priest in the sense that it is more to give Our Savior his human nature than to make His body present in the Blessed Eucharist.* Mary has given us the Priest of the sacrifice of the Cross, the Principal Priest of the sacrifice of the Mass and the Victim offered on the altar.[66]

Because of her divine maternity, Mary's heart beats with mercy for each priest without exception. Although some priests have no particular devotion to Mary, this does not preclude her devotion to them. Once a young priest confided to me that he had no devotion to Mary because he had suffered very much in his lifetime, and he thought Mary could not relate to his suffering because she was preserved from pain by a special grace from God. Only after reading the popular book *33 Days to Morning Glory*[67] did his heart break open to let Mary inside because he came to know the extent of Mary's suffering. The priest was transformed when he let Mary into his priesthood for the first time. His strained relationship with his earthly mother was subsequently healed.

Since Mary participated in the immolation of Jesus the High Priest, she understands everything about the priest and assists him in his own process of sanctification. Is the maternal heart of Mary really capable of anything less?

---

[66] Fr. Reginald Garrigou-Lagrange, O.P., *Mother of the Savior and Our Interior Life* (Charlotte, NC: TAN Books, 1993), 184, emphasis added.

[67] Michael E. Gaitley, M.I.C., *33 Days to Morning Glory* (Stockbridge, MA: Marian Press, 2011).

Mary, Priests, and Spiritual Motherhood

Mary: Mother of Priests

Priests are often referred to as sons of the Virgin Mary. The most joyful priests I have met are those who consecrate themselves to Mary and relate to her as a son. She is the *perfect* Mother of all Catholic priests because she is the Mother of the Eternal High Priest.

Fr. Peter Cameron, O.P., explains, "Despite the excellence of our mothers, we persist nonetheless in looking for that *ultimate* maternal mirror in which we can discover ourselves to our deepest depths. Mary's is the face we seek."[68] Why? Pope Benedict XVI explains the reason we need her help: "We can only love ourselves if we have first been loved by someone else. The life a mother gives to her child is not just physical life; she gives total life when she takes the child's tears and turns them into smiles. It is only when life has been accepted and is perceived as accepted that it becomes also acceptable."[69] We can understand now why "Mary's is the face we seek" as the "ultimate maternal mirror" and why she helps us know that we are lovable. In a distinct way Mary does this for priests.

We see a recent and vivid example of Mary's maternity of priests in the pontificate of Pope John Paul II, who chose *Totus tuus* ("totally yours") as his papal motto. When the Polish pope spiritually encountered Mary during the Second World War, he wrote, "I was convinced that Mary leads us to Christ, but at that time I began to realize also that Christ leads us to his mother."[70]

---

[68] Peter Cameron, O.P., *The Mysteries of the Virgin Mary* (Cincinnati: Servant Books, 2010), 61.

[69] Ibid.

[70] Karl Wojtyla, quoted by Hayden Williams, O.F.M. Cap., *Serving the Love of Loves* (Malta: Outlook Coop., 2011), 174.

Praying for Priests

Most people are aware that Pope John Paul II credited Mary's intercession for sparing his life when four bullets from a would-be assassin struck him while he was blessing pilgrims in St. Peter's Square on May 13, 1981. A year to the day later, the pope placed one of those bullets in Mary's crown at the Shrine of Our Lady of Fátima in Portugal. This leaves little doubt as to the real and powerful grace of Mary's maternity toward priests.

The renowned Mariologist Fr. Emile Neubert, S.M., in his wonderful book *Mary and the Priestly Ministry*, helps us to understand Mary's spiritual maternity, which stems from her "cooperation in the mysteries of the Incarnation, the Redemption, and the distribution of grace."[71] Let us note how Mary, in these three functions, becomes the Mother of priests:

1. The *Incarnation* sets special grounds for Mary's motherhood of priests. Mary provided the material cause of Christ's priesthood. Mary then carried all her Son's future priests in her womb along with Him. She did not know them individually at that time, but she wished for them what Jesus wished for them at that time, and loved them with the same special love her Son had for them.

2. Our Mother Mary's special role in the *Redemption*: If Mary, in the Incarnation, conceived us spiritually, as it were, then in the mystery of the Redemption she gave us birth. At the foot of the Cross, Christ confided Mary to John, who was a priest, and it is to priests, above all, that Christ gives His Mother because He has a greater love for them and they have a greater need of her.

---

[71] Fr. Emile Neubert, S.M., *Mary and the Priestly Ministry* (New Bedford, MA: Academy of the Immaculate, 2009), 8.

3. Our Mother Mary's special role in the *distribution of grace*: Mary has a special love for priests: if maternity consists essentially in giving and in nurturing life, can any human maternity be understood apart from such a love? Mary loves all the faithful with incomparable love. But she loves priests with an altogether unique love because she sees in the priest a greater resemblance to the image of her Son than in any other Christian of equal holiness.

Fr. Neubert also gives us five reasons for Mary's special love for priests:

1. She sees in the priest a greater resemblance to the image of her Son than in any other Christian of equal holiness.

2. Jesus loves His priests with a distinctive love. Mary shares all the feeling of her Son.

3. It is thanks to priests, above all, that the work of Christ is carried out in the world.

4. In her union with her Son, she foresaw especially those who would continue His mission on earth.

5. She needs priests. It is especially through them that she can carry out her mission of giving Jesus to the world.[72]

Let us consider the way that Mary exemplifies spiritual maternity of priests, and the scope of priestly masculinity and feminine complementarity. Alice von Hildebrand addresses this eloquently: "How beautiful is the complementariness of men

---

[72] Ibid., 8-17.

and women according to the Divine Plan. It is not by accident that St. Francis of Assisi was best understood by St. Clare; St. Francis of Sales by St. Jeanne Francoise de Chantal; St. Vincent de Paul by Louise de Marillac."[73]

In 2008, Fr. John Cihak gave an inspired presentation entitled "The Blessed Virgin Mary's Role in the Celibate Priest's Spousal and Paternal Love"[74] at Mount St. Mary's Seminary in Emmitsburg, Maryland. It is now distributed to diocesan seminarians and priests who receive instruction at the Institute for Priestly Formation in Omaha, Nebraska. I encourage readers to consult the document online for a better understanding of spiritual motherhood.[75]

Particularly insightful are Fr. Cihak's suggestions regarding the four major dimensions of priestly masculinity and feminine complementarity; they help us see the ordered structure of Marian spiritual motherhood.

Fr. Cihak writes:

In the order of nature, we can begin to see the importance of women in the development of the priest as a man: his mother and his sisters help to lead him into maturity as a good son and brother. A man's relationship with his mother begins *in utero* where as son he begins to become

---

[73] Alice Von Hildebrand, *The Privilege of Being a Woman* (Ann Arbor: Sapientia Press, 2005), 47.

[74] Fr. John Cihak, S.T.D., "The Blessed Virgin Mary's Role in the Celibate Priest's Spousal and Paternal Love," presented at the Bicentennial Marian Symposium at Mount St. Mary's Seminary, Emmitsburg, Maryland, October 9-11, 2008.

[75] This document can be accessed online for free at www.ignatiusinsight.com/features2009/jcihak_maryandpriests1_july09.asp.

attuned to his mother, her heartbeat, her bodily processes, her movements, her emotions; we could say even her soul. In infancy, it is hoped, at some point the mother's smile awakens him to self-consciousness. Her smile gives him his awareness in the midst of her feminine love that he is a unique person. The beauty, goodness, and truth evinced in the mother's smile awakens in the child an awareness of the beauty, goodness, and truth of the world, and by analogy, of God.

Psychiatry and neurobiology describe this as a process of "secure (healthy) attachment," a subtle attunement between mother and child which is essential for normal brain and psychological development, as well as normal spiritual development, especially in those crucial first five years of life. This relationship continues in childhood where a boy continues to learn how to be a son and eventually a brother. In all of this development the mother's (and sisters') role is neither as an object to be used, nor as being overprotective or cultivating a "womanish" affect in her son—all of which would be a collapsing of the masculine-feminine complementarity. The healthy son or brother does not identify with the mother or sister in such a way that he imitates her femininity (e.g., in imitating effeminate characteristics himself); rather, he relates to her as truly an "other" with whom he, in his masculinity, can relate through a process of complementary, self-giving love.

... In the life of grace, we immediately grasp Our Lady's role in helping a man be a good son.

... This complementary engagement of the Blessed Virgin Mary's feminine love with the priest's masculine love happens within the central mystery of the priesthood: the Cross, and specifically in the scene of Our Lady and St. John at the foot of the Cross.[76]

This reminds me of a story I once heard. A very old priest was close to death. Some friends asked a nun from a local convent to help look after the infirm priest, and she cheerfully did so. During her daily visits, she helped the old priest in every way possible, always trying to bring joy to his routine and simply to keep him company. After a few weeks, the priest said to her, "All of my life, I have tried to avoid women, since I am a priest. But in these last weeks that you have visited me, I see that I unnecessarily deprived myself of the grace of friendships that would have enriched my priesthood. But I am grateful to have learned this now, rather than not to have known this gift at all."

That we might better understand and appreciate the essence of spiritual motherhood of priests, we can also reflect upon Jesus's act of entrusting His Mother Mary and John the Beloved to each other. Fr. Cihak, drawing from this scene at the foot of the Cross, continues developing the idea of the complementarity of the feminine heart of Mary, which calls forth the best of the masculine heart of John for their mutual support:

> I like to meditate on that scene, pondering the eyes of Our Lady and St. John as they meet in their mutual agony. Neither of them seems to have Jesus anymore. At that moment she needs St. John; she also allows him to help her. She is so alone at the moment. She who is sinless allows her great poverty of spirit to need this man and priest

[76] Cihak, "The Blessed Virgin Mary's Role in the Celibate Priest's Spousal and Paternal Love."

beside her. Her feminine complementarity draws out the best in St. John's masculine heart. The need for his support and protection must have connected to something deep within him as a man. How does he help her? St. John says that he then took her "into his own" (in Greek, *eis ta idia*). What does this mean? "His house," as many translations read? "His things"? What about "everything that he is"? Perhaps it indicates that he takes her into his life as a priest.

She also is supporting him. He is depending on her in that moment for he too is so alone. I wonder if he felt abandoned by the other apostles. She leads the way in sacrificing herself, for her feminine heart is more receptive and more attuned to Jesus's. She is not only present but leads the way for him, helping the priest to have his own heart pierced as well. There is much here to ponder as she engages his masculine love. He gives himself over to her, to cherish her and console her. At this moment she needs him and needs him to be strong, even if she is the one really supporting him.

The Blessed Virgin Mary's role is to call out of the priest this celibate *agape* to help him become a husband to the Church and a spiritual father — a strong father, even in his weakness. She does this at the Cross by drawing the priest out of his own pain to offer pure masculine love in the midst of her own pure feminine love. This scene becomes an icon of the relationship between the priest and the Church. The priest hands himself over to the Church in her suffering and need — to have his life shaped by hers. At the foot of the Cross the Church agonizes in labor to give birth to the members of the mystical body.[77]

The DNA of the Incarnate Word remains with Mary just as the DNA of any child remains with his mother.[78] But Mary's Child is the Eternal High Priest sent by the Father for the redemption of humanity. Mary's heart goes out to the priest because she sees the indelible image of the Eternal High Priest that was conferred upon him by the sacrament of Holy Orders. She who was mystically crucified with Jesus is mystically united to the priest by an act of God's will to which she is completely surrendered.

Mary knows the priest earnestly needs a mother — just as Jesus needed His Mother to fulfill His mission. The Son became dependent upon the Mother's yes at the Incarnation, and the Mother was dependent upon the Son's yes for her redemption. What she did for Jesus on earth she does for the priests who continue the unbroken lineage of the Eternal High Priest. She loves, encourages, protects, feeds, embraces, cleans, delights, teaches, and keeps him company. She who did not leave her Son at the foot of the Cross remains with the priest for his singular mission. Mary saw the truth of the Crucifixion, and she knows how to lead the priest to victory through the Cross.

Love compelled the Mother to enter into the sacrifice of the Son so she could experience the mystical crucifixion of each

---

[77] Cihak, "The Blessed Virgin Mary's Role in the Celibate Priest's Spousal and Paternal Love."

[78] Nancy Shute, "Beyond Birth: A Child's Cells May Help or Harm the Mother Long after Delivery," *Scientific American*, April 30, 2010, accessed October 15, 2013, www.scientificamerican.com/article.cfm?id=fetal-cells-microchimerism.

priest chosen to imitate Christ. Mary assists the priest in the refinement of his will, in the purification of his heart, in the conformity of his mind to God. Mary aids the priest in living chastely and growing in charity, wisdom, and fortitude for a martyrdom of love. She who experienced the mystical Crucifixion of Jesus will help each priest to do the same for the joy of the kingdom of God.

The priest needs the love of Mary's feminine heart to bring him to the fulfillment of the masculine ideal in order to protect humanity from all that is harmful. Jesus, the New Adam, is the Redeemer and protector of the human family. The priest is the protector of all that belongs to Christ: men, women, and children, heaven and earth. The priest is at his best when, like Christ, he guards the dignity and vocation of every man, woman, and child.

Mary is God's guardian of the priest's dignity and vocation. The Mother gently moves him to be transfigured into Christ. Through the maternal mediation of Mary, the priest becomes the sacrifice that offers the perfect Sacrifice; the priest becomes the love that offers Love.

Mary: Icon of Spiritual Motherhood

Jesus once made a very sobering assertion to Ven. Conchita: "Priests must go to heaven, and not alone, but with a retinue of souls saved by their conduct; and how many also go to hell dragging many souls condemned by their sin!"[79] Jesus reminds us of His affliction over the fall of priestly souls, and surely the heart of Mary grieves over this as well. Jesus's assertion speaks

---

[79] A Mis Sacerdotes, 111 (text translated by John Nahrgang).

to the reality of spiritual battle in the life of priests. This is why the Holy See is urgently calling us to strengthen the ministerial priesthood. Matthew's Gospel reminds us: "For it is written, 'I will strike the shepherd, and the sheep of the flock will be scattered'" (Matt. 26:31).

Spiritually placing ourselves and priests under the mantle of Mary is not a magical formula, but it is a remedy for our time when done as part of an authentic consecration to the Immaculate Heart of Mary. In practical terms, it means, "I'm Mary's child." Or as a priest recently said at a conference, "I'm Mary's problem—not my own!" This priest was truly free of himself!

Mary's spiritual motherhood is addressed in the *Catechism*:

> This motherhood of Mary in the order of grace continues uninterruptedly from the consent which she loyally gave at the Annunciation and which she sustained without wavering beneath the cross, until the eternal fulfillment of all the elect. Taken up to heaven she did not lay aside this saving office but by her manifold intercession continues to bring us the gifts of eternal salvation.... Therefore the Blessed Virgin is invoked in the Church under the titles of Advocate, Helper, Benefactress, and Mediatrix.[80]

The mystical piercing of Mary's heart was silent and hidden and was for the sake of an unending joy that would follow. The Gospels never record a verbal protest, argument, or any other kind of resistance from the Mother of Jesus. Hers is the perfect imitation of her Son, of whom it is written, "Like a lamb that is led to the slaughter, and like a sheep that before its shearers is dumb, so he opened not his mouth" (Isa. 53:7). Mary's silence

---

[80] *Lumen Gentium*, no. 62, quoted in CCC, no. 969.

speaks volumes about the depth of a human anguish within the soul that is too profound for words. With that silence comes all the concentration of her heart to be completely surrendered. Her broken heart becomes a portal through which St. John and every priest thereafter can enter to receive the consolation of Marian charity and strength.

In one of his homilies, Pope Francis spoke in practical terms about Mary's spiritual motherhood, stating the current situation in the world and the need for her maternity toward souls:

> Mary is the mother, and a mother worries above all about the health of her children, she knows how to care for them always with great and tender love. Our Lady guards our health. What does this mean? I think above all of three things: she helps us grow, to confront life, to be free.
>
> 1. A mother helps her children grow up and wants them to grow strong; that is why she teaches them not to be lazy — which can also derive from a certain kind of wellbeing — not to sink into a comfortable life-style, contenting oneself with possessions. The mother takes care that her children develop better, that they grow strong, capable of accepting responsibilities, of engaging in life, of striving for great ideals. The Gospel of St Luke tells us that, in the family of Nazareth, Jesus "grew and became strong, filled with wisdom; and the favor of God was upon him" (Luke 2:40). Our Lady does just this for us, she helps us to grow as human beings and in the faith, to be strong and never to fall into the temptation of being human beings and Christians in a superficial way, but to live responsibly, to strive ever higher.

2. A mother then thinks of the health of her children, teaching them also *to face the difficulties of life*. The mother helps her children to see the problems of life realistically and not to get lost in them, but to confront them with courage, not to be weak, and to know how to overcome them, in a healthy balance that a mother "senses" between the area of security and the area of risk. And a mother can do this! She does not always take the child along the safe road, because in that way the child cannot develop, but neither does she leave the child only on the risky path, because that is dangerous. A mother knows how to balance things. A life without challenges does not exist and a boy or a girl who cannot face or tackle them is a boy or girl with no backbone!

3. Lastly, a good mother not only accompanies her children in their growth, without avoiding the problems and challenges of life; a good mother also helps them *to make definitive decisions with freedom*. This is not easy, but a mother knows how to do it. But what does freedom mean? It is certainly not doing whatever you want, allowing yourself to be dominated by the passions, to pass from one experience to another without discernment, to follow the fashions of the day; freedom does not mean, so to speak, throwing everything that you don't like out the window. No, that is not freedom! Freedom is given to us so that we know how to make good decisions in life! Mary as a good mother teaches us to be, like her, capable of making definitive decisions; definitive choices, at this moment in a time controlled by, so to speak, a philosophy of the provisional. It is very difficult to make a lifetime commitment. And she helps us to make those definitive

decisions in the full freedom with which she said "yes" to the plan God had for her life (cf. Luke 1:38).[81]

The simple yet profound terms that Pope Francis uses to express Mary's universal motherhood remind me of my own mother. I was blessed to have a devoted mother who exemplified maternal charity, encouraged my siblings and me, and taught us the importance of discipline, excellence, self-sacrifice, and reliance on God's providence. She modeled for us the freedom of a simple life and love for family and neighbor. She always opened her doors to neighbors who sought her compassion and sage advice. She had the wisdom of a godly woman.

The test of authentic motherhood is fruitful service, not selfish covetousness. Motherhood is about remembering to be true to the feminine ideal of *receptivity* that always makes room for the other. These terms sound very sacrificial, and they are. But every mother learns that the travail of birthing something beautiful is worth it! It is a matter of love that flowers naturally like a rose that is rooted in earthly soil but blooms by sunlight and water. A mother's love grows out of the feminine heart attuned to the Sacred and Immaculate Hearts. The feminine heart needs to drink deeply of divine love to become a living spring like Mary's.

The greatest of all maternal loves is that of the Virgin Mary, Mother of Jesus! Mary's maternal love always magnifies the Lord, always proclaims His marvelous deeds, always remembers what God has done and always rejoices in being chosen to serve. I believe Mary's perpetual *Magnificat* is a hymn she desires

---

[81] Pope Francis, Address at the Basilica of St. Mary Major, Rome, May 3, 2013.

to inscribe on the heart of every believer so that the Church may form one united chorus of praise and gratitude, affirming, "He has mercy on those who fear him in every generation" (Luke 1:46-55). The motherhood of Mary is always fruitful in service to the glory of God. She is our heavenly Mother, perpetually engaged in forming other mothers to whom life can be entrusted — physical and spiritual — because maternal love is always abundantly creative.

Another icon of Mary's motherhood that is greatly venerated, especially in the Americas, is Our Lady of Guadalupe. Her iconic words to St. Juan Diego reflect a sublime and merciful maternal love:

> Hear and understand, my smallest and dearest son, that what is alarming and afflicting you is nothing. Do not let your countenance or your heart be disturbed. Do not fear this illness or any other illness or suffering. Am I, your Mother, not here? Are you not under my shadow and protection? Am I not the source of your joy? Are you not in the folds of my mantle, in the crossing of my arms? What more do you need?[82]

These words are a healing balm for every child of Mary. Who are the children of Mary? God gave Mary to *all His children*! In Mary, everyone finds the perfect maternal love that brings out the best in us.

But there is a deeper way of abiding in the Immaculate Heart — through Marian consecration. St. Louis de Montfort

---

[82] Our Lady of Guadalupe to Juan Diego, quoted in Paul Badde, *María of Guadalupe: Shaper of History, Shaper of Hearts* (San Francisco: Ignatius Press, 2008), 33-34.

and St. Maximilian Kolbe have spread the glories of Marian consecration throughout the Church.[83] Pope Pius XII defines consecration in this way:

> Consecration to the Mother of God is a total gift of self, for the whole of life and for all eternity; and a gift which is not a mere formality or sentimentality, but effectual, comprising the full intensity of the Christian life — Marian life. This consecration tends essentially to union with Jesus, under the guidance of Mary.[84]

The work of Christ in the Church is always magnified through the heart of Mary. To live Marian consecration is to live Christ, since their two hearts are bound in one love.

We have been given a great confirmation of the efficacy of Marian consecration in recent times through Pope Francis's consecration of the entire world to Mary on October 13, 2013. When the Vicar of Christ dedicates the world to Mary, it reflects a great need for maternal intervention to help us reorder our lives to God.

Who doesn't need the Mother of God to advocate for him? And who would choose to live without the consolation of Mary's company and help? And who would refuse to join in her maternal mission of saving souls? To be consecrated to Mary is to be set apart for a sacred purpose. One who is set apart for a

---

[83] Two wonderful contemporary books on Marian consecration are Fr. Michael Gaitley's *33 Days to Morning Glory* (Stockbridge, MA: Marian Press, 2011) and Fr. Brian McMaster's *Totus Tuus: A Consecration to Jesus through Mary with Blessed John Paul II* (Huntington, IN: Our Sunday Visitor, 2013).

[84] Pope Pius XII, Consecration to the Immaculate Heart of Mary, October 31, 1942.

sacred purpose is under the mantle of grace. A holy alliance, a covenant, is forged when a person offers himself to God through Mary. A covenant is a profound reality in the spiritual realm. A communion exists between Mary and her consecrated children so she can act freely and gloriously on their behalf.

But Mary never acts independently of her Spouse, the Holy Spirit. Yes, God willed that Mary and the Holy Spirit be espoused. The great St. Louis de Montfort helps us to understand the significance of this:

> To Mary his faithful spouse, God the Holy Spirit has communicated his unspeakable gifts; and he has chosen her to be the dispenser of all he possesses, in such wise that she distributes to whom she wills, as much as she wills, as she wills and when she wills, all his gifts and graces. The Holy Spirit gives no heavenly gift to men which he does not have pass through her virginal hands. Such has been the will of God, who has willed that we should have everything through Mary; so that she who, impoverished, humbled, and who hid herself even unto the abyss of nothingness by her profound humility her whole life long, should now be enriched and exalted and honored by the Most High. Such are the sentiments of the Church and holy Fathers.[85]

Since this book deals with the sanctification of priests, and the laity who pray for them, it is important to understand how Mary and the Holy Spirit work together to sanctify souls. Jesus was conceived by the Holy Spirit and born of the Virgin Mary. We know this since it is part of our Creed.

---

[85] St. Louis de Montfort, *True Devotion to Mary*, no. 25.

Mary, Priests, and Spiritual Motherhood

Archbishop Luis María Martínez teaches:

That is the way Jesus is always conceived. That is the way He is reproduced in souls. He is always the fruit of Heaven and earth. Two artisans—the Holy Spirit and the most holy Virgin Mary—must concur in the work that is at once God's masterpiece and humanity's supreme product. Both the Holy Spirit and the Virgin Mary are necessary to souls, for they are the only ones who can reproduce Christ....

These two, then, the Holy Spirit and Mary, are the indispensable artificers of Jesus, the indispensable sanctifiers of souls. Any saint in Heaven can cooperate in the sanctification of a soul, but his cooperation is not necessary, not profound, not constant. But the cooperation of these two artisans of Jesus of whom we have just been speaking is so necessary that, without it, souls are not sanctified (and this by the actual design of Providence), and so intimate that it reaches to the very depths of our soul.... Such is the place that the Holy Spirit and the Virgin Mary have in the order of sanctification.[86]

Archbishop Martínez helps us to understand that we need to invoke Mary *and* the Holy Spirit, since they are the two artisans who conceive Jesus in a soul. Mary and the Holy Spirit *always* work together. They are the agents of the New Evangelization. The sanctification of priests is *their joint mission.*

---

[86] Luis M. Martínez, *True Devotion to the Holy Spirit* (Manchester, NH: Sophia Institute Press, 2000), 8-9. Archbishop Martínez was Archbishop of Mexico from 1937 until his death in 1956.

Praying for Priests

Mary's spiritual motherhood of humanity did not begin at the foot of the Cross when Jesus said to John, "Behold, your Mother" (John 19:27). Mary's spiritual maternity began when the Holy Spirit overshadowed her at the Incarnation, according to Fr. Neubert, who states, "In the mystery of the Incarnation, Mary becomes the Mother of all the faithful, because in giving life to our Head, she simultaneously gave it to all the members of the Mystical Body of Christ."[87]

Spiritual Motherhood of Priests

In this book, it is my ardent desire to encourage my sisters in Christ to consider that just as priests participate in the eternal priesthood of Jesus Christ, women can also participate in the spiritual motherhood of priests in union with Mary, Icon of Spiritual Maternity. St. Edith Stein (also known by her religious name, Teresa Benedicta of the Cross) movingly describes how this is possible:

> The *intrinsic value of woman* consists essentially in *exceptional receptivity for God's work in the soul.*[88]

For an understanding of our unique feminine nature, let us look to the pure love and spiritual maternity of Mary. This spiritual maternity is the core of a woman's soul. Wherever a woman functions authentically in this spirit of maternal pure love, Mary collaborates with her. This holds true whether the woman is married or single, professional or domestic or both, a Religious in the world or in the convent. Through this love, a woman is God's special

[87] *Mary and the Priestly Ministry*, 10.
[88] St. Edith Stein, *Essays on Woman* (Washington, D.C.: ICS Publications, 1996), 259.

weapon in His fight against evil. Her intrinsic value is that she is able to do so because she has a special susceptibility for the works of God in souls—her own and others. She relates to others in His spirit of love.[89]

Here St. Edith Stein helps women understand the feminine heart, which is somewhat mysterious even to women. The quotation has striking points worthy of deep reflection. I have always marveled at the capacity of a woman's heart to be engaged in the art of loving.

In the course of speaking at many Magnificat chapter gatherings over the years, I have heard the powerful testimonies of countless women. Their stories are heartrending dramas of the triumph of maternal love over sometimes terrifying circumstances. There is something great at work in the maternal heart that helps a woman to rise to occasions requiring her steadfast love.

A very feminine image comes to me now: that of a pregnant womb. I think the feminine heart is something like that when it is exercising maternal love—it expands to include everyone who needs her love. As St. Edith Stein teaches, this is because women have a "special susceptibility for the works of God in souls—hers and others." Women have a God-given spiritual intuition ordered to the work of divine love. God created women to be life-bearers, and this is a distinct dignity. Whether the life we bear is spiritual or physical, or both, we are called to be bearers of the Word of God for others in emulation of Mary.

The Church recognizes the need for spiritual motherhood and acknowledges the unique dignity of the maternal-feminine

[89] St. Edith Stein, quoted by Freda Mary Oben in *The Life and Thought of St. Edith Stein* (New York: Alba House, 2001), 82.

heart. On December 8, 1965, at the closing of the Second Vatican Council, the Council Fathers said, "At this moment when the human race is undergoing so deep a transformation, women impregnated with the spirit of the Gospel can do much to aid mankind in not falling." The word *impregnated* is not accidental. It indicates that women allow the gospel to take hold of their hearts and take root in their minds so as to be able to give the gift they have received to others. This sounds like a tall order! But let us recall St. Edith Stein's words: "Wherever a woman functions authentically in this spirit of maternal pure love, Mary collaborates with her." We have God's Mother to "mother" us in the art of spiritual motherhood.

Mary is always at the service of God and His people, especially His priests. The Congregation for the Clergy's initiative of spiritual maternity rightly points out that the spiritual motherhood of priests is "a hidden vocation, invisible to the naked eye."[90] They invite women disciples to imitate Mary in her maternal motherhood. I know holy women to whom priests confide their deep need for prayer. Not a word is ever spoken to anyone about this while the spiritual mother prays and suffers for the priest's intention, winning grace for his priesthood. This is authentic spiritual motherhood of priests. The charism of spiritual maternity of priests can be a vocation within a vocation and can be lived by people of all walks of life.

A woman who is called to spiritual maternity of priests should first be schooled in the virtues of the Mother of the Eternal High Priest. She must be thoroughly Marian in character, thought, word, and deed. She should have spent hours of reflection with

---

[90] *Eucharistic Adoration for the Sanctification of Priests and Spiritual Maternity*, 12.

Mary to learn from her how to pray for priests—never assuming that she knows how to pray, but always aware that she must be led by the Holy Spirit, who led Mary to pray and serve.

To the priest, she should bring the face and heart of Mary and no other agenda. It was Mary's self-effacement that made it possible for her to magnify the Lord. To magnify Jesus with Mary is to participate in her spiritual motherhood of priests.

In preparation for writing this book, I asked some priests at an international conference about their impressions of spiritual motherhood. Some negative impressions surprised me. Whether this was a reaction to adverse experiences of well-intentioned women who had overstepped boundaries, I do not know.

In contrast, I think of the humble first words of the newly elected Pope Francis when he implored the world, "Pray for me." Telling indeed are these words, uttered as they were in the first moments of his pontificate. Are they not the cry of a humble heart in reverence of his office? "Pray for me" is the cry of the Christian grounded in an ordered self-knowledge. St. James writes, "Therefore confess your sins to one another, and pray for one another, that you may be healed. The prayer of a righteous man has great power in its effects" (James 5:16). The closer our relationship with God becomes, the more we are aware of the need for the prayers of others.

There seems to be a lack of understanding about what comprises authentic spiritual maternity for priests. An authentic spiritual mother can only be a gift to the priest. I believe the majority of priests acknowledge this and deeply appreciate the prayers and sacrifices of spiritual mothers.

I once asked some Catholic women at a conference about their ideas concerning spiritual maternity. It was my impression that praying for priests was at the periphery of their lives due to other demands on their time and resources. In their defense, catechesis on Catholic womanhood and spiritual maternity has been lacking. In a recent interview, Pope Francis said, "A profound theology must be made of woman."[91]

I have been edified by the generosity of women offering prayer and sacrifice for priests through Marian apostolates such as Magnificat, Women of Grace, and Endow.[92] I have been especially blessed by the stellar examples of Sr. Briege McKenna and Fr. Kevin Scallon, C.M., Magnificat's international spiritual director. Intercession for priests is indeed an ecclesial undertaking well under way in the life of the Church, yet there is so much more to be done!

At a recent social gathering, I asked some parents if their Catholic schools had priests or nuns teaching or visiting the students. I apparently opened a can of worms, because I received complaints about the absence of priests and nuns in Catholic schools. I then asked if they ever had a conversation with their sons or daughters concerning the possibility of a vocation to the priesthood or religious life. They readily admitted never having had such a conversation, and some quickly added that they did not want their children to become priests or nuns. This group had their children in Catholic schools.

Such situations confirm what is written in the Congregation for the Clergy's booklet:

[91] Quoted in "Pope Francis' Press Conference on Return Flight from Brazil (Part 2)" (transcript), Zenit, August 2, 2013, accessed November 30, 2013, http://www.zenit.org/en/articles/francis-press-conference-on-return-flight-from-brazil-part-2.

[92] For information on these apostolates, visit their websites: Magnificat: www.magnificat-ministry.org; Women of Grace: www.womenofgrace.com; Endow: www.endowgroups.org.

Mary, Priests, and Spiritual Motherhood

The vocation to be a spiritual mother for priests is largely unknown, scarcely understood and, consequently, rarely lived, notwithstanding its fundamental importance. It is a vocation that is frequently hidden, invisible to the naked eye, but meant to transmit spiritual life....

The present situation of the Church in a secularized world and the subsequent crisis of faith has the pope, bishops, priests, and faithful looking for a way forward. At the same time, it is becoming increasingly clear that the real solution lies in the interior renewal of priests, and in this context the so-called "spiritual maternity of priests" assumes a special role. Through being "spiritual mothers", women and mothers participate in the universal motherhood of Mary, who as mother of the Supreme and Eternal High Priest, is also the mother of all priests of all times.

If in natural life a child is conceived, born, nurtured and cared for by its mother, then this applies even more to the spiritual life: behind all priests there is a spiritual mother who asked God for their vocation. She bears them through spiritual suffering and "nourishes" them by offering to God all her daily activities, so that they become holy priests, priests faithful to their special identity and special commitments.[93]

The booklet *Eucharistic Adoration for the Sanctification of Priests and Spiritual Maternity* emphasizes several crucial points about the priesthood and women in the Church:

[93] *Eucharistic Adoration for the Sanctification of Priests and Spiritual Maternity*, 12-13.

- The Church's way forward in addressing a crisis of faith in a secularized world is through *the interior renewal of priests.*

- *Women participate in the universal motherhood of Mary.*

- "Spiritual maternity of priests" assumes a special role in this renewal.

- A spiritual mother bears priests through spiritual suffering and "nourishes" them by offering to God all her prayers, sufferings, and even ordinary daily activities.

- A spiritual mother thus helps them become holy priests who are faithful to their special identity.

Women who place themselves at the service of God and the Church will find the Holy Spirit and Mary inviting them to engage in spiritual motherhood of priests for the salvation of souls. God has formed feminine hearts to be able to say yes to His holy prerogatives. Women who choose Mary as their model of discipleship will become like our Mother in fruitfulness through *obedient* service to the Church, beginning with praying for priests. It was to John the apostle that she first extended her spiritual motherhood. The Holy Spirit within Mary directed her charity to him and to all priests, and the Holy Spirit within Marian women will do the same and bring about an ever-greater impulse for spiritual maternity of priests—through holy obedience and love.

When Fr. Cantalamessa gave his testimony at the Grapevine, Texas, Magnificat chapter, he said to the seven hundred women in attendance, "Go, and be the apostle to the Apostles!" I believe this is what the Congregation for the Clergy is asking of us today by inviting women of the Church to become spiritual mothers of priests. It prompts me to visualize St. Mary Magdalene as an "apostle to the apostles," since she wholeheartedly placed herself at the service of Mary and priests.

Let us do likewise! Let us pray:

> *Mary, graciously pray for your*
> *daughters, and help us to pray*
> *for priests as you do.*
>
> *Mary, you are God's living letter*
> *of maternal love. Help your daughters to read*
> *your Immaculate Heart so that we may be*
> *schooled in the art of spiritual maternity.*
> *Then, having received the same*
> *Holy Spirit that overshadowed you,*
> *send us forth from your Immaculate Heart*
> *to be your ambassadors as spiritual mothers*
> *of priests for the New Evangelization. Amen.*

4

๛

Heroines of Spiritual Maternity

In the history of the Church, even from earliest times,
there were side-by-side with men a number of women,
for whom the response of the Bride to the Bridegroom's
redemptive love acquired full expressive force.[94]

—St. John Paul II

The saints who lived the charism of spiritual maternity teach us the beauty of interceding for our shepherds. Women of faith have greatly enriched the Church through lives totally dedicated to interceding for priests.

A great example of such a spiritual heroine is St. Faustina Kowalska, who records this in her spiritual diary:

> On one occasion I saw a servant of God in the immediate danger of committing a mortal sin. I started to beg God to deign to send down upon me all the torments of hell and all the sufferings He wished if only this priest would be set free and snatched from the occasion of committing

---

[94] *Mulieris Dignitatem*, no. 27

a sin. Jesus heard my prayer and, that very instant, I felt a crown of thorns on my head. The thorns penetrated my head with great force right into my brain. This lasted for three hours; the servant of God was set free from this sin, and his soul was strengthened by a special grace of God.[95]

God so loved the priest who was going to fall into sin that He inspired a humble nun to make an offering of herself on behalf of this shepherd! The measure of St. Faustina's charity for priests seemed boundless, but it was costly. The extent of her suffering was probably unique, and yet I sense that other consecrated brides of Christ in this very time are enduring such suffering for priests with the same generosity. While heaven alone has the consolation of seeing the hidden labor of the brides of Christ, the universal Church experiences the fruit of their sacrifice in marvelous ways.

The testimonies of past heroines of prayer are not only edifying but also instructive. Following are profiles of both well-known and unsung heroines who beautifully witnessed to the charism of spiritual maternity of priests. Most of these testimonies have been excerpted with gratitude from the Congregation for the Clergy's 2012 booklet, which beautifully articulates the lives of these heroines of prayer so we can see how they brought forth incredible, lasting fruit that can inspire a new generation of prayer warriors for priests.

St. Monica (331-387): laywoman, wife, and mother

St. Monica is a famous example of a mother's intercession for her son. After his radical conversion of heart, St. Augustine

[95] *Diary of St. Maria Faustina Kowalska: Divine Mercy in My Soul* (Stockbridge: Marian Press, 1987), no. 41.

praised his mother's untiring intercession with words of ardent charity: "For love of me, she cried more tears than a mother would over the bodily death of her son. Nine years passed in which I wallowed in the slime of that deep pit and the darkness of falsehood. Yet that pious widow desisted not all the hours of her supplications, to bewail my case unto Thee where her prayers entered into Thy presence."[96]

After his conversion, he said thankfully, "My holy mother never abandoned me. She brought me forth in her flesh that I might be born to this temporal light, and in her heart, that I might be born to life eternal. I have my mother to thank for what I have become and the way that I arrived there!"[97] Through the ages, Catholic mothers and wives have taken St. Monica as their patron and inspiration. I implored her help quite often in the raising of my sons and was always strengthened by her example.

St. Catherine of Siena (1347-1380): single laywoman

Catherine was holy from her youth, and at the age of six she had a mystical experience of Jesus that forever changed her life. Her maternal love embraced priests through her constant intercession for them. She even became a spiritual mother to Pope Gregory XI, and in 1376 she persuaded him to move the entire Papal Court back to Rome from Avignon, France.

On one occasion, Catherine wrote the following to the Dominican friar Bl. Raymond of Capua, her spiritual director:

---

[96] St. Augustine, quoted in *Eucharistic Adoration for the Sanctification of Priests and Spiritual Maternity*, 11.
[97] Ibid., 15.

I've heard ... that you have been experiencing tremendous struggles and that your spirit has been overtaken by darkness because of the devil's illusions and deceits. He wants to make you see the crooked as straight and the straight as crooked, and he does this to make you stumble along the way so you won't reach your goal. But take heart. God has provided and will continue to provide for you, and his providence will not fail you. See that in everything you turn to Mary as you embrace the cross. And don't ever give in to spiritual discouragement, but navigate the stormy sea on the ship of divine mercy.[98]

St. Catherine died at the age of thirty-three and was declared a Doctor of the Church[99] in 1970 by Pope Paul VI.

Eliza Vaughan (d. 1853): laywoman, wife, and mother

Eliza Vaughan came from a strong Protestant family, which helped found the Rolls-Royce car company. Yet even during her childhood education in France, she was deeply impressed by the exemplary efforts of the Catholic Church in caring for the poor.

After she married Colonel John Francis Vaughan in the summer of 1830, Eliza converted to the Catholic Faith, despite the objection of her relatives. During the Catholic persecution in England under Queen Elizabeth I (1558-1603), the Vaughans' ancestors preferred imprisonment and expropriation to being unfaithful to their beliefs.

---

[98] *The Letters of Catherine of Siena*, vol. II, trans. Suzanne Noffke (Tempe, AZ: Medieval & Renaissance Studies, 2001), 473.

[99] This honor has been awarded by the Church to only thirty-five individuals for making great contributions to Catholic doctrine or theology.

Heroines of Spiritual Maternity

During the decades of terror in England, Courtfield, the ancestral family home, became a refuge for priests, a place where the Holy Mass was often celebrated secretly. Nearly three centuries had now passed, but the Catholic beliefs of the family had not changed.

So profound and zealous was Eliza's religious conversion that she proposed to her husband to offer all of their children back to God. This remarkable woman made a habit of praying for an hour each day before the Blessed Sacrament in the house chapel at Courtfield. She prayed to God for a large family and for many religious vocations among her children. And her prayers were answered! She bore fourteen children and died shortly after the birth of the last child, John, in 1853.

Of the thirteen children who lived, six of her eight boys became priests; two priests in religious orders, one diocesan priest, a bishop, an archbishop, and a cardinal. Of her five daughters, four became nuns in religious orders. What a blessing for the family, and what an impact on all of England!

Two months after Eliza's death, Colonel Vaughan wrote in a letter that he was convinced divine providence had brought Eliza to him: "I thanked the Lord in adoration today that I could give back to him my dearly beloved wife. I poured out my heart to him, full of thankfulness that, as an example and a guide, he gave me Eliza with whom I am still now bound by an inseparable, spiritual bond. What wonderful consolation and grace she brought me! I still see her as I always saw her before the Blessed Sacrament: her inner purity and extraordinary human kindness which her beautiful face reflected during prayer."[100]

---

[100] *Eucharistic Adoration for the Sanctification of Priests and Spiritual Maternity*, 18-19.

Praying for Priests

Bl. Maria Deluil Martiny (1841-1884): religious sister

Approximately 120 years ago, Jesus began to reveal His plan for the renewal of the priesthood to consecrated women living in and out of convents. He entrusted this so-called Priest Work to spiritual mothers.

Bl. Maria Deluil Martiny is a precursor of this work for priests. Regarding this great intention of her heart, Mother Maria Deluil Martiny said, "To offer yourself for souls is beautiful and great ... but to offer yourself for the souls of priests is so beautiful, so great, that you would have to have a thousand lives and offer your heart a thousand times.... I would gladly give my life if only Christ could find in priests what he is expecting from them. I would gladly give it even if just one of them could perfectly realize God's divine plan for him!"

She did, in fact, seal her priestly motherhood with the blood of martyrdom at age forty-three. Her last words were, *"This is for the work, for the Priest Work!"*[101]

St. Thérèse of Lisieux (1873-1897): religious sister

The Little Flower, as St. Thérèse is lovingly called, is a renowned spiritual mother of priests. One of my favorite books, *Maurice and Thérèse: The Story of a Love*, contains the inspiring letters between a struggling young priest and this young nun. Sr. Thérèse once wrote the following to Fr. Maurice while he was out in the mission fields:

> It must be that you don't know me at all well, if you are afraid that a detailed account of your faults could lessen

---

[101] *Eucharistic Adoration for the Sanctification of Priests and Spiritual Maternity*, 21.

the tenderness that I feel for your soul! O my brother, believe me that I shall not need to "put my hand over the mouth of Jesus," He has forgotten your infidelities long ago. Only your desires for perfection remain to make His heart rejoice. I implore you, don't drag yourself to His feet ever again. Follow that first impulse which draws you into His arms."[102]

We can imagine the consolation this message brought! Here we see exemplified the genius of Thérèse—complete confidence in God's love and mercy.

The Congregation's booklet highlights a story from her life that reveals the depths of a love ready to suffer for priests:

On a pilgrimage to Rome, when she was only fourteen years old, Thérèse came to understand her vocation to be a spiritual mother for priests. In her autobiography she describes that after meeting many holy priests on her trip to Italy, she understood their weaknesses and frailty in spite of their sublime dignity. "*If holy priests . . . show in their conduct their extreme need for prayers, what is to be said of those who are tepid?*" In one of her letters she encouraged her sister Céline, "*Let us live for souls, let us be apostles, let us save especially the souls of priests . . . let us pray, let us suffer for them, and, on the last day, Jesus will be grateful.*"

In the life of Thérèse, Doctor of the Church, there is a moving episode which highlights her zeal for souls, especially missionaries. While she was very ill and had great difficulty walking, the nurse advised her to take a little walk

[102] Patrick Ahern, *Maurice and Thérèse: The Story of a Love* (New York: Image Books, 1998), 188-189.

in the garden for a quarter of an hour each day. She obeyed faithfully, although she did not find it effective. On one occasion, the sister accompanying her noticed how painful it was for her to walk and remarked, "*You would do better to rest; this walking can do you no good under such conditions. You're exhausting yourself.*" The saint responded, "*Well, I am walking for a missionary. I think that over there, far away, one of them is perhaps exhausted in his apostolic endeavors, and, to lesson his fatigue, I offer mine to God.*"[103]

Thérèse's heart, aflame with divine love, intercedes for all souls but especially for priests. These words from young Fr. Maurice, written to his beloved Sr. Thérèse near the time of her death, demonstrate the impact of her loving heart:

Let us adore God, Sister. Thank Him with me. This love of God almost scares me. Nonetheless I hope that confidence will win out and make me give myself completely. This above all is asked of me. My spiritual Father has said to me: "You must give yourself completely to God, Who asks that you give Him everything. You cannot serve Him by halves. You will either be a good priest or you will never amount to anything." That is my own feeling, and I want to give without counting the cost, being very sure that "when somebody loves he does not calculate," so that when I set foot on the soil of Africa I'll be able to continue with the words: "I have given all. I run with a light heart. I have nothing anymore except my only riches, namely, To Live by Love."[104]

---

[103] *Eucharistic Adoration for the Sanctification of Priests and Spiritual Maternity*, 34.

[104] *Maurice and Thérèse*, 117-118.

Heroines of Spiritual Maternity

Ven. Louise Margaret Claret De La Touche (1868-1915): religious sister

Over the course of many years, Jesus prepared the Ven. Louise Margaret Claret de la Touche for her apostolate for the renewal of the priesthood. The Lord appeared to her on June 5, 1902, while she was in adoration:

> "Praying to him for our little novitiate, I asked him to give me some souls I might form for him. He replied: 'I will give you the souls of men.' Being profoundly astonished by these words, the sense of which I did not understand, I remained silent ... until Jesus said: 'I will give you the souls of priests.' Still more astonished I asked him: 'My Jesus how will you do that?' ... Then he showed me that he has a special work to do, which is to enkindle the fire of love again in the world, and that he wished to make use of his priests to accomplish it. He said to me: 'Nineteen centuries ago, twelve men changed the world; they were not merely men, but they were priests. Now, once more twelve priests could change the world ... but they must be holy.'" Subsequently, the Lord let Louise Margaret see the outcome of the Work. "'It is a special union of priests, a Work, which encompasses the whole world.... Priests who will form part of this work will undertake, among other things, to preach Infinite Love and mercy, but first his heart must be penetrated by Jesus and enlightened by his spirit of love. They must be one heart and one soul, and never impeding one another in their activities.'"

Louise Margaret wrote so impressively about the priesthood in her book *The Sacred Heart and the Priesthood* that priests believed the anonymous writer to be a fellow priest. A Jesuit even exclaimed, "I do not know who wrote this book, but one thing I do know, it is not the work of a woman!"[105]

The Mothers of Lu

The little village of Lu, in northern Italy, is located in a rural area 90 kilometers east of Turin. It would still be unknown to this day if some of the mothers of Lu had not made a decision that had important consequences in 1881.

The deepest desire of many of these mothers was for one of their sons to become a priest or for a daughter to place her life completely in God's service. Under the direction of their parish priest, Msgr. Alessandro Canora, they gathered every Tuesday for adoration of the Blessed Sacrament, asking the Lord for vocations. They received Holy Communion on the first Sunday of every month with the same intention. After Mass, all the mothers prayed this prayer together:

> O God, grant that one of my sons may become a priest!
> I myself want to live as a good Christian and want
> to guide my children always to do what is right,
> so that I may receive the grace, O God, to be
> allowed to give you a holy priest! Amen.

Through the trusting prayer of these mothers, and the openness of the other parents, an atmosphere of deep joy and Christian piety developed in the families, making it much easier for the children to recognize their vocations. Still, no one expected

---

[105] *Eucharistic Adoration for the Sanctification of Priests and Spiritual Maternity*, 21.

that God would hear the prayers of these mothers in such a dramatic way.

From the tiny village of Lu came 323 vocations: 152 priests (diocesan and religious) and 171 nuns belonging to forty-one Congregations. In some cases, several vocations came from a single family. The most famous example is the Rinaldi family, from whom God called seven children. Two daughters became Salesian sisters, both of whom were sent to San Domingo as missionaries. Five sons became priests, all joining the Salesians.[106]

Berthe Petit (1870-1943): single laywoman

As a fifteen-year-old girl, Berthe began praying at every Holy Mass for the celebrant: *"My Jesus, do not allow your priests to displease you!"* When she was seventeen, her parents lost everything they had in a failed business venture. On December 8, 1888, Berthe's confessor explained to her that her vocation was not to enter a convent but to stay at home and care for her parents. Although she accepted this sacrifice with a heavy heart, Berthe asked for a zealous and holy priest in place of her religious vocation. "You will certainly be heard!" assured her confessor.

She could not have known what would take place just sixteen days later: A twenty-two-year-old lawyer, Dr. Louis Decorsant, was praying before a statue of the Sorrowful Mother. Unexpectedly he had an inner certainty that it was not his vocation to take the girl he loved to be his wife and to establish himself as a notary. He understood very clearly that God was

---

[106] *Eucharistic Adoration for the Sanctification of Priests and Spiritual Maternity*, 22-23.

calling him to be a priest. The call was so clear and urgent that he did not hesitate to give up everything. Upon finishing his studies and doctorate in Rome, he was ordained to the priesthood in Paris in 1893. At the time, Berthe was twenty-two years old.

On Christmas that year, the newly ordained twenty-seven-year-old priest celebrated Midnight Mass in a church outside Paris. Berthe was participating in Midnight Mass in another church, and she solemnly promised the Lord, "Jesus, I will be a sacrifice for the priests, for all priests, but especially for the priest in my life."

During exposition of the Blessed Sacrament, Berthe suddenly saw Jesus hanging on the Cross and Mary and John standing beneath it. Then she heard the words, "Your offer has been accepted, your prayer heard. Behold your priest ... you will be able to meet him one day." And Berthe saw that John's features resembled a priest, but one she did not know. This priest was none other than Fr. Decorsant, whom she would recognize at their first encounter—some fifteen years later, in 1908.

Berthe made a pilgrimage to Lourdes, where the Blessed Virgin confirmed, "Now you will see the priest whom you asked God for twenty years ago; you will meet him soon." That same year, she made another trip by train to Lourdes, this time with a friend of hers. A priest got on at the station in Paris, trying to find a place for a sick woman. It was Fr. Decorsant. His features were those that Berthe had seen on St. John's face fifteen years earlier. She had prayed frequently and offered all of her physical suffering for him. After a couple of friendly words, he left the compartment.

One month later, Fr. Decorsant also made a pilgrimage to Lourdes because he wanted to entrust the future of his priesthood to our Lady. With suitcases in hand, he met Berthe and her friend. Recognizing the two women, he invited them to Holy Mass. When Fr. Decorsant elevated the Host, Jesus interiorly said to Berthe, "This is the priest for whom I accepted your sacrifice."

After the Holy Mass, Berthe was surprised to see that the "priest of her life," as she called him from then on, was staying in the same hotel as they were. Shortly thereafter, Berthe was able to speak to him about her interior life and another mission that was entrusted to her — the promulgation of the consecration to the Immaculate and Sorrowful Heart of Mary. Fr. Decorsant felt that this precious soul had been entrusted to him by God. He accepted a position in Belgium and became a holy spiritual director for Berthe Petit as well as an untiring support for the realization of her mission. Theologically sound, he was the ideal person to maintain a correspondence between Berthe and the hierarchy of the Church in Rome. For twenty-four years until his death, he accompanied Berthe Petit in her expiatory vocation; she was often very sick and suffered especially for priests who had left the priesthood.[107]

Servant of God Consolata Betrone
(1903-1946): religious sister

The sacrifices and prayers of a spiritual mother for priests benefit especially those who have strayed or abandoned their vocations. Jesus has called countless women in His Church to this vocation of prayer, such as Sr. Consolata Betrone, a Capuchin nun from Turin. Jesus said to her, "Your lifelong task is for your brothers. Consolata, you, too, shall be a good

---

[107] *Eucharistic Adoration for the Sanctification of Priests and Spiritual Maternity*, 26-27.

shepherdess and go in search of your brothers and bring them back to me."

Consolata offered everything for "her brother" priests and others consecrated to God who were in spiritual need. While working in the kitchen, she prayed continuously in her heart, *"Jesus, Mary, I love you; save souls!"* She consciously made every little service and duty into a sacrifice. Jesus said in this regard, "Your duties may be insignificant, but because you bring them to me with such love, I give them immeasurable value and shower them on the discontented brothers as grace for conversion."

Very grave and difficult cases were often entrusted to the prayers of the convent. Consolata would take the corresponding suffering upon herself. For weeks or months on end she sometimes endured dryness of spirit, abandonment, meaninglessness, inner darkness, loneliness, doubt, and the sinful state of the priests.

She once wrote to her spiritual director during these struggles, "How much the brothers cost me!" Yet Jesus made her a magnificent promise: "Consolata, it is not only one brother that you will lead back to God, but all of them. I promise you, you will give me the brothers, one after another." And so it was! She brought back all of the priests entrusted to her to a fulfilling priesthood. There are recorded testimonies of many of these cases.[108]

Bl. Alexandrina da Costa (1904-1955): single laywoman

A story from the life of Alexandrina da Costa, beatified on April 25, 2004, reveals the transforming power and visible effects of the sacrifice made by a sick and forgotten girl.

---

[108]*Eucharistic Adoration for the Sanctification of Priests and Spiritual Maternity,* 25.

In 1941, Alexandrina wrote to her spiritual director, Fr. Mariano Pinho, telling him that Jesus told her, "My daughter, a priest living in Lisbon is close to being lost forever; he offends me terribly. Call your spiritual director and ask his permission that I may have you suffer in a special way for this soul."

Once Alexandrina had received permission from her spiritual director, she suffered greatly. She felt the severity of the priest's errors, how he wanted to know nothing of God and was close to self-damnation. She even heard the priest's full name. Poor Alexandrina experienced the hellish state of this priest's soul and prayed urgently, "Not to hell, no! I offer myself as a sacrifice for him, as long as you want."

Fr. Pinho inquired of the cardinal of Lisbon whether one of the priests of his diocese was of particular concern. The cardinal openly confirmed that he was, in fact, very worried about one of his priests, and when he mentioned the name of the priest, it was the same name that Jesus had spoken to Alexandrina.

Some months later, a friend of Fr. Pinho, Fr. David Novais, recounted to him an unusual incident. Fr. David had just held a retreat in Fátima , and one of the attendees was a modest gentleman whose exemplary behavior made him pleasantly attractive to all the participants. On the last night of the retreat, this man suddenly had a heart attack. He asked to see a priest, to whom he confessed and received Holy Communion. Shortly thereafter he died, fully reconciled with God. It turned out that this man was actually a priest—the very priest for whom Alexandrina had suffered so greatly.[109]

---

[109] Ibid., 24.

Praying for Priests

Mother Judith Zuniga, O.C.D.: religious sister

Dear reader, divine providence has a wonderful way of crossing our paths with people whom the Lord has chosen to become part of our spiritual family. I am grateful for the day two priest friends invited me to join them for a visit with Mother Judith Zuniga, O.C.D., Superior General of the Carmelite Sisters of the Most Sacred Heart of Los Angeles. Over lunch, I observed the joy of these three servants of the Church as they shared stories of their time together in Rome, where they had met and studied. I realized that I was witnessing spiritual maternity in action.

I present Mother's testimony below for your edification. She was hesitant at first out of humility, but the Holy Spirit had His way! The history of the Carmelites is replete with spiritual heroines of prayer for priests. Mother Judith continues this tradition today. I'm grateful that she is now my spiritual mother also.

༈

A number of years ago, I had the immense privilege to study and work in Rome. It was during those very blessed years that our Lord granted me the grace-filled opportunity to meet wonderful priests and seminarians whose enduring friendships would serve to deepen my respect and love for the sacred priesthood of Jesus Christ. As I studied and worked alongside these very dear spiritual sons and brothers, their joys, accomplishments, sorrows, and struggles became my very own, and it was through them, by them, in them, and for them that I came to understand and appreciate more profoundly my own role as spiritual mother of priests.

How does one begin to verbalize a matter of the heart such as the spiritual maternity of priests? As a Carmelite Sister, I treasure it from the core of my being as a sacred gift that has been entrusted to me.

The realities of spiritual paternity and spiritual maternity are inextricably grounded in the sacrament of Baptism, since, by virtue of our Baptism in Christ, we are made collaborators in His plan of redemption for the salvation of souls.

A baptized Catholic who is genuinely serious about his relationship with Jesus Christ must necessarily cultivate an interior life of prayer in order for this friendship (or bond) to grow and deepen. Charity, good example, and self-sacrifice for the material and spiritual well-being of others are concrete expressions of the fruitfulness of genuine prayer and a loving union with Christ. Thus, a true disciple of Jesus Christ must be attentive to nurturing and strengthening the spiritual life of others. There can be no genuine interior life or sanctity in a soul in which the actualization of spiritual paternity or spiritual maternity is lacking.

In the Gospel of Matthew, Christ tells us that "whoever does the will of my Father in heaven is my brother, and sister, and mother" (12:50). In explaining this passage, Pope John Paul II noted that our Lord wanted us to understand that motherhood "is always related to the Covenant which God established with the human race through the motherhood of the Mother of God." Then, with specific reference to motherhood, the Holy Father stated, "The motherhood of every woman, understood in the light of the Gospel, is similarly not only 'of flesh and blood': it expresses a profound 'listening to the word of the living God' and a readiness to 'safeguard' this Word, which is 'the word of eternal life' (cf. Jn 6:68)."[110]

A spiritual mother, like Mary, is always ready at any cost to safeguard the word of God. In this way, she becomes a personification of Mary, the Mother of God. A spiritual mother, through her own sacrifices, prayers, and works of charity for the sanctification of others, acts *in persona Matris*. A spiritual mother must have not only a profound union with Christ, but also a deeply personal relationship with His beloved Mother. Indeed, spiritual motherhood is truly a very lofty vocation offered to all baptized women who wholeheartedly live out their baptismal consecration.

Spiritual maternity toward priests in particular is profoundly Marian. Just as Mary was devoted to Her Son, the Great High Priest, so, too, spiritual mothers after her own heart are particularly solicitous for the spiritual well-being of those souls Christ Himself has chosen to be *alteri Christi* through the ministerial priesthood.

The unique bond between priest and "spiritual mother" is both tender and intensely powerful. How often I have heard priests speak affectionately of their spiritual mothers, grateful to them for nurturing the priestly vocation that had stirred within them as youngsters and faithfully nurturing that vocation with constant prayer, loving sacrifice, and wise counsel through their seminary days and beyond ordination. I have witnessed elderly priests who still gratefully recall the names of the religious sisters who

[110] Pope John Paul II, *Mulieris Dignitatem*, no. 19.

taught them in elementary school and encouraged them to embrace their priestly vocation.

Several years ago, one of our Sisters celebrated her seventy-fifth anniversary in religious life. One of her former second-grade students, an archbishop, flew down to concelebrate the Mass of Thanksgiving. When he came up to greet Sister, she immediately beamed and with gentle maternal affection said, "Hello, Frankie!" as she had called him in grammar school. At that moment, smiles and tears comingled among those present for the ceremony! It was a beautiful and tangible reminder among the faithful of what spiritual maternity of priests looks like!

In the history of the Church, countless saintly women have ministered to priests in imitation of Mary. Out of all the Gospel passages that mention these women, the Gospel reading that the Church places on the feast of Our Lady of Mount Carmel is that of Mary accompanying Jesus at the foot of the Cross. It is a poignant reminder of our Carmelite charism to support priests by our prayers and sacrifices.

When St. Teresa of Ávila initiated her reform of the Carmelite order, it was for the purpose of praying for the needs of the Church and for priests. The Church in her time was being torn asunder by the Protestant Reformation, and St. Teresa was determined to do what she could to help the Church and priests. In *The Way of Perfection*, she counsels her spiritual daughters that they must "help our King" (Christ) by helping those He has chosen, "these servants of God who at the cost of so much toil, have fortified themselves with learning and virtuous living and have labored to help the Lord."[111]

She goes on to explain to her Sisters:

> Therefore there are two things you must try to obtain from God, and live in such a way as to be worthy to do this. First, that there will be many of these very learned and religious men who have the qualifications for their task; and that the Lord will prepare those who are lacking in anything. One who is perfect will do more than many who are not. Second, that the Lord may have them in His hand so that they may be delivered from all the dangers that are in the world.... Pray especially for kings and prelates of the Church, especially for the bishop; remember that if you have a prelate who is holy, those who live under him will be holy too. Recommend him continually to the Lord. If your prayers and desires and disciplines and fasts are not performed for the intentions of which I have spoken, you are not carrying out the work or fulfilling the object for which the Lord has brought you here.[112]

The saints of Carmel have left us many reflections regarding our obligation to be spiritual mothers for priests by our constant prayers for them.

In *The Story of a Soul*, St. Thérèse of the Child Jesus reiterated this vital mission of Carmel of praying for priests

---

[111] St. Teresa of Ávila, *The Way of Perfection* (Sydney: E. J. Dwyer, 1988), 10.
[112] *The Way of Perfection*, 12-13.

when telling her prioress of the trip to Rome she had made with her father and sisters before entering Carmel:

> For a month I lived with many holy priests, and I saw that if their sublime dignity raised them above the angels, they are nonetheless weak and fragile men.... If holy priests whom Jesus calls in the Gospel "the salt of the earth" show in their behavior that they have an extreme need of prayers, what can one say about the ones who are lukewarm? Didn't Jesus add, "But if the salt loses its saltiness, how can it be made salty again?" (Mt. 5:13)?
>
> Oh Mother! How beautiful is the vocation that has as its object to preserve the salt that is destined for souls! That vocation is Carmel's, since the only objective of our prayers and sacrifices is to be the apostle of the apostles, praying for them while they evangelize souls through their words and especially by their examples.[113]

Carmel's love of the priesthood was expressed by St. Teresa of the Andes, a young Chilean Carmelite, when she wrote:

> The goal the Carmelite proposes to herself is very great: to pray and sanctify herself for sinners and for priests. To become holy so that the divine sap be communicated, by the union that exists between the faithful and all the members of the

---

[113] St. Thérèse of Lisieux, *Story of A Soul* (Brewster, MA: Paraclete Press, 2006), 134.

Church. She immolates herself on the cross, and her blood falls on sinners, imploring mercy and repentance for them. It falls on priests to sanctify them since on the cross she's intimately united with Jesus Christ. Her blood then is mixed with the divine.[114]

The Carmelite is the sister of the priest. Both offer a host of holocaust for the salvation of the world.... In a word, she sanctifies herself to sanctify her brothers.[115]

A young French Carmelite, Blessed Elizabeth of the Trinity, understood her apostolic work of prayer and sacrifice to be associated with the work of the priest and said, "The life of a priest—and that of a Carmelite—is an advent which prepares the way for the Incarnation in souls."[116]

To me, as a Carmelite Sister of the Most Sacred Heart of Los Angeles, praying for priests is as vital as breathing! To pray for my brothers "out in the trenches" is not only a great gift given to me, but also an immense responsibility that I do not take lightly. In fact, praying for priests is

[114] St. Teresa of the Andes, quoted in Michael Griffin, O.C.D., *Testimonies to Blessed Teresa of the Andes* (Washington, D.C.: Teresian Charism Press, 1995), 104-105.

[115] Quoted in Griffin, *Testimonies to Blessed Teresa of the Andes*, 107.

[116] Blessed Elizabeth of the Trinity, quoted in Conrad de Meester, ed., *I Have Found God: Complete Works*, vol. 2 (Washington, D.C.: ICS Publications, 1995), 232-233.

of primary importance in our Congregation, and this is clearly expressed in our constitutions.

Our Congregation was founded in Mexico in the early 1920s during a fierce and horrific religious persecution. Our Mother Foundress, Ven. Mother María Luisa Josefa of the Most Blessed Sacrament (affectionately known as Mother Luisita), and our founding Sisters experienced the pain, fear, and suffering of seeing priests hunted down, captured, and executed simply for being priests. They witnessed priests risking their lives to come to them to celebrate Holy Mass. Churches had been closed, and any religious education or celebration was forbidden by law.

On December 24, 1928, Mother Luisita made an offering of herself to God:

Lord, do me the charity of accepting me as Your own; I do not have any of the virtues required for You to accept me, but look at Your own merits and my desires. Here I am, Lord. I offer myself to You without any reservations or conditions. I want to deny You nothing. Deign to accept me so that once and for all I am in right relationship with You. I am here. I am Yours. Do with me as You will. Give me Your love, and make me suffer whatever You like and in whatever manner You want....

If You are pleased with my life, here it is, Lord, any way You want it.

Without breaking the fulfillment of my vows, I offer myself and all of my life to You for sinners in atonement for the sins that are committed every day and for priests.

My Jesus, give me the necessary strength to suffer whatever You want to give me.... Even though
my desire is that my life will be consumed soon,
and how I wish I could hasten its coming, yet I
resign myself to Your holy will.

My Lord, I promise You to accept gladly any
interior sorrow, sickness, contempt, calumny, false
testimony, and my life, whatever way You are
pleased to have me.

And if my sufferings have any merit, I offer
them for priests and in a very special way for my
Sisters.

Every December 24, we Sisters gratefully recount
Mother Luisita's offering for the priesthood and for her
Sisters.

Mother Luisita, like the two great reformers of Carmel, St. Teresa of Ávila and St. John of the Cross, left
us a tender example of the efficacy of spiritual maternity.
Fr. Pedro of St. Elías (Heriz) was a Carmelite priest from
Spain who was sent to Mexico, then to the United States,
and ultimately returned to his homeland. Our archives
are blessed to have twenty-four extant letters from Father
written to Mother Luisita during the years 1927 to 1932.
The letters begin with the salutation, "My Dear Mother"
or "Dear Mother in Christ" or "Esteemed Mother." The
signature is always preceded by "Your devoted brother in
Christ."

Although no existing letters from Mother Luisita
have been found to date, she often speaks of him in her
writings and encourages prayers for him. In one letter,

written while she was in the United States as a refugee from religious persecution in Mexico, she writes: "About Father Pedro, in my opinion he should be canonized upon his death. How good he is and what a great interest he takes in us."

Mother's words were prophetic. Fr. Pedro was martyred in Spain in 1936 during the persecution of the Church at that time. On October 13, 2013, he was beatified along with many other martyrs of that sad time.

Mother Luisita herself is a candidate for sainthood and was declared Venerable by Pope John Paul II on July 1, 2000. These two great souls leave us an eloquent example. Like St. Paul writing to the Corinthians, they become to one another a "letter from Christ" mutually supporting one another on their journey to their true homeland.

Yes, our Congregation's personal history of religious persecution impels us to cherish a very deep love, respect, and gratitude for the priesthood of Jesus Christ. We are doubly grateful for this history as well as for the spiritual tradition of the Discalced Carmelites we have received from our Holy Mother, St. Teresa of Ávila.

I can think of no better way to conclude this brief reflection on spiritual maternity for priests than to use a prayer composed by St. Thérèse of Lisieux:

Prayer for Priests

O Jesus, Eternal Priest,
keep Your priests within
the shelter of Your Sacred Heart,
where none may touch them.

Keep unstained their anointed hands,
which daily touch Your Sacred Body.

Keep unsullied their lips, daily purpled
with Your Precious Blood.

Keep pure and unworldly their hearts,
sealed with the sublime mark
of Your priesthood.

Let Your holy love surround
them from the world's contagion.

Bless their labors with abundant fruit,
and may the souls to whom they minister
be their joy and consolation here
and their everlasting crown hereafter.

Mary, Queen of the Clergy, pray for us;
obtain for us numerous and holy priests.[117]

---

[117] Quoted in Norma Cronin Cassidy, ed., *Favorite Novenas and Prayers* (New York: Paulist Press, 1990), 113-144.

5

⳹

The Holy Hour: An Encounter with Jesus

To contemplate the face of Christ, and
to contemplate it with Mary, is the "program"
which I have set before the Church
at the dawn of the third millennium, summoning
her to put out into the deep on the sea of history
with the enthusiasm of the new evangelization.[118]

—St. John Paul II

The initiative of prayer for priests calls for deepening our encounter with Jesus the Eternal High Priest through worship of Him in the Eucharist. We in the Church must quicken our response to the universal call to holiness. We must persevere to become holy in a culture that is quite unholy and swiftly succumbing to the profane. What is needed is a radical conversion of Eucharistic amazement resulting from an encounter with omnipotent Love. We can then discover the secret of the Divine Presence that remains with us and is *the cure* for what

---

[118] *Ecclesia de Eucharistia*, no. 6

ails humanity. St. Josemaría Escrivá wrote of this abiding presence that we encounter in the Eucharist:

> Think of the human experience of two people who love each other, and yet are forced to part. They would like to stay together forever, but duty—in one form or another—forces them to separate. They are unable to fulfill their desire of remaining close to each other, so man's love—which, great as it may be, is limited—seeks a symbolic gesture. People who make their farewells exchange gifts or perhaps a photograph with a dedication so ardent that it seems almost enough to burn that piece of paper. They can do no more, because a creature's power is not as great as its desire. What we cannot do, our Lord is able to do. Jesus Christ, perfect God and perfect man, leaves us, not a symbol, but a reality. He himself stays with us. He will go to the Father, but he will also remain among men. He will leave us, not simply a gift that will make us remember him, not an image that becomes blurred over time, like a photograph that soon fades and has no meaning except for those who were contemporaries. Under the appearances of bread and wine, he is really present, with his body and blood, with his soul and divinity.[119]

In my travels to seminaries and Magnificat chapters in the United States and abroad, I have discovered among many Catholics a deep sense of privation, a longing in the human heart—a sense of absence and even estrangement from true communion with God. This is a paralyzing reality among believers. How can

[119] Josemaría Escrivá de Balaguer, *Christ Is Passing By* (Chicago: Scepter Press, 1990), 121-122.

this be when Jesus is *always and truly present* in the Eucharist, on the altars and in the tabernacles of the world? Jesus hasn't abandoned us; He is truly and perpetually present! Often we claim to be looking for God, but our back is turned to Him as we look to people and places where God is not found. We have to turn around to look at Jesus—face-to-face in the Eucharist—to make sense of the madness of the world all around us.

There is a *great thirst* among God's people, but the thirst of Jesus is far greater. The Heart of the Eternal High Priest is not fickle like the human heart. The Church's initiatives, including the crusade of prayer for priests, will be fruitful only if we fall in love with Jesus in the Eucharist. The Eucharist is the deepest, most life-changing encounter with Jesus the High Priest!

The name *Jesus the Eternal High Priest* is intimately related to *His hour* when in Gethsemane Jesus prayed to the Father and to His perfect sacrifice on the altar of the Cross. Jesus is our High Priest, the victim of His own intercession for sinners. Scripture describes Jesus as a priest in this way:

> Since then we have a great high priest who has passed through the heavens, Jesus, the Son of God, let us hold fast our confession. For we have not a high priest who is unable to sympathize with our weaknesses, but one who in every respect has been tempted as we are, yet without sinning. Let us then with confidence draw near to the throne of grace, that we may receive mercy and find grace to help in time of need. (Heb. 4:14-16)

The Eternal High Priest is a "victim offering" to God the Father for the ransom of humanity. Each ministerial priest becomes a victim offering also. Archbishop Fulton Sheen eloquently writes about this to his brother priests:

That moment when the priest lifts up the Host and the Chalice, he is at his best. A bride and groom are at their peak of loveliness and lovability at the moment of marriage. Love is said to be blind because it sees no faults in the beloved. God's love becomes blind at this moment. He sees us through "the rose-colored glasses" of his Son. Never again will we appear as priestly, as victimal, as deserving of salvation, as we are when the Father sees us through "the rose-colored glasses" of the Body and Blood of his Son as we lift Host and Chalice to heaven. During this holy action, we priests become holy (Exodus 39:29). But we are also victims. We do not just *offer* Mass; we are also *offered*.[120]

If we take time to ponder these sublime truths of our Faith, we are struck with awe at the gift of God. He loved us into being, ransomed us from sin and death by laying down His life so that we can live forever, and then perpetuates Himself in the ministerial priesthood so that we can encounter the living Jesus made present by His priests.

The letter to the Hebrews says, "Since then we have a great high priest who has passed through the heavens, Jesus, the Son of God, let us hold fast our confession." What does it mean to hold fast our confession? We confess that Jesus is Lord; we confess our faith in and love for Christ. We bear witness by our life and our good works. How can our confession of faith and love for Jesus be convincing if we are not encountering him? The Holy Hour is one way to encounter Jesus personally.

---

[120] Fulton Sheen, *Those Mysterious Priests* (Staten Island, NY: Alba House, 2005), 159-160, emphasis added.

The Holy Hour: An Encounter with Jesus

In its 2012 booklet, the Congregation for the Clergy included a suggested protocol for *public or parish* observance of a Holy Hour.[121] In many areas of the world, Eucharistic adoration is not readily available to the faithful. Therefore, I offer this chapter inviting everyone to pray (as often as possible) a *private* Holy Hour before the tabernacle in their church to encounter Jesus, to deepen their personal relationship with Him, and to participate in the mission of interceding for priests and vocations.

Fr. Raniero Cantalamessa illustrates how Eucharistic adoration can be an individual or group experience:

> Eucharistic adoration may be personal or communal; in fact, it expresses the full force of what it signifies when an assembly is before the Blessed Sacrament, singing, praising, or simply kneeling. This invitatory psalm, with which the Liturgy of the Hours opens every day, aptly expresses the shared character of adoration: "O come, let us worship and bow down, let us kneel before the Lord, our Maker!" (Psalm 95:6).[122]

The Holy Hour is meant be to an encounter with the living Jesus. It is an exercise of love, not a project to be accomplished. One hour with the Divine Sacrament will improve the quality of the remaining twenty-three. Communing with the Divine Lover of our soul becomes irresistible joy, not labor. The words of Bl.

---

[121] *Eucharistic Adoration for the Sanctification of Priests and Spiritual Maternity*, 43-47.

[122] Raniero Cantalamessa, *This Is My Body: Eucharistic Reflections Inspired by* Adoro Te Devote *and* Ave Verum (Boston: Pauline Books and Media, 2005), 25.

Teresa of Calcutta inspire us: "When you look at the Crucifix, you understand how much Jesus loved you then. When you look at the Sacred Host you understand how much Jesus loves you now."[123] I've been experiencing this love of Jesus for twenty-three years, ever since I began making a daily Holy Hour.

Some may be wondering if there is a formula the Church recommends for making a Holy Hour. In the guidance I've received from my spiritual directors over the years, and in reflecting on my own experience with Eucharistic adoration, I humbly submit to you the following recommendations:

- Come into Jesus's presence with expectant faith and humility.

- Greet Jesus with honor, praise, and gratitude.

- Try to recollect yourself by reading a psalm or another Scripture passage or praying the holy Rosary.

- Offer prayers of petition.

- Allow ample time to listen in silence.

- Contemplate Jesus, His life, and His teaching.

- Rest in the silent presence of Jesus.

- Receive the love and inspiration that He wants to give you.

- Encounter Jesus personally in an intimate relationship of love.

[123] Quoted in *At the Altar of the World: The Pontificate of Pope John Paul II through the Lens of L'Osservatore Romano and the Words of Ecclesia de Eucharistia* (Washington, D.C.: Pope John Paul II Cultural Center, 2003), 170.

If you fall asleep, think of how a medical surgeon puts his patient under anesthesia so he can operate on him while he is unconscious. Jesus can operate on your soul in a similar manner while you rest or even sleep! Do not be anxious about the right or wrong formula or prayers, but show reverence and docility to the way that Jesus moves your heart. Cultivate a listening heart. Jesus is pleased to have your company!

Let us also consider the wisdom of Archbishop Sheen as he addresses priests regarding how to make a Holy Hour. This advice can easily apply to laypeople as well:

> No rules — just spend a continuous hour before the Blessed Sacrament. If however, a part of the hour were made before Mass and the rest of it after Mass, that would still be continuous.
>
> Sometimes it is hard, especially during vacations when we have nothing to do. I remember having two hours between trains in Paris. I went to the Church of St. Roch to make my Holy Hour. There are not ten days a year when I can sleep in the daytime. This was one. I was so tired, I sat down at 2:00 p.m. — too tired to kneel, and went to sleep. I slept perfectly until 3:00 p.m. I said to the Good Lord: "Did I make a Holy Hour?" The answer came back: "Yes! That's the way the Apostles made their first one." The best time to make it is in the morning, early, before the day sets traps for us.[124]

Earlier in his book *Those Mysterious Priests*, Archbishop Sheen does recommend that we make a Holy Hour at a time when we are fresh for the Lord and able to be alert to His interior

---

[124] *Those Mysterious Priests*, 193.

promptings. Occasionally, if we are sleepy during our Holy Hours, we should not lose our peace of soul. After all, does a loving parent get upset when his little child falls asleep in his arms? God is our loving parent. But it's also true that parents enjoy seeing their children when they're alert!

Encountering Jesus through Intercessory Prayer

When we pray for priests and vocations, or ask anything on behalf of another, we petition God the Father through the intercession of the Eternal High Priest. As I grew closer to Jesus through a deepening prayer life, I became attuned to the intentions of His priestly Heart.

Prayer is always powerful, but intercessory prayer is uniquely aligned to the heart of the Eternal High Priest, who now lives at the right hand of the Father, interceding for the human family. Prayer changes situations, and it transforms human hearts. Prayer not only draws graces on the priest or the person for whom we are praying; it also draws grace into the hearts of us pray-ers who offer petitions to God in faith, with love and hope.

Prayer is meant to be a *personal encounter* with Jesus. The splendors of the Eucharist and the glories of the Eternal High Priest are as lofty as the heavens and as infinite as divine love. We are invited to rediscover the sublime beauty of the love of Jesus that remains with us in the Sacred Host. We need to rediscover the gift of God in the Eucharist to rediscover the gift of the priest, who makes Jesus present there.

Encountering Jesus through Eucharistic Amazement

In 2003, Pope John Paul II laid out a plan for the New Evangelization that starts with contemplating the face of Christ. Less than five years later, Cláudio Cardinal Hummes, then prefect for the Congregation for the Clergy, invoked Mary in a letter to bishops around the world, inviting them to further Pope John Paul II's program via Eucharistic adoration:

> By becoming her children, we learn the true meaning of life in Christ. Thereby—and precisely because of the role of the Most Blessed Virgin in salvation history—we intend to entrust in a very particular way all priests to Mary, the Mother of the Eternal High Priest, bringing about in the Church *a movement of prayer, placing 24-hour Eucharistic adoration at the center, so that prayers of adoration, thanksgiving and praise, petition and reparation will be raised to God, incessantly and from every corner of the earth, with the primary intention of awakening a sufficient number of holy vocations to the priestly state, while at the same time spiritually and maternally uniting—at the level of the Mystical Body—all those who have already been ontologically conformed to the one Eternal High Priest through the ministerial priesthood.* This movement will offer better service to Christ and his brothers—those who are both "inside" the Church and "at the forefront" of the Church, standing in Christ's stead and representing him, as head, shepherd and spouse of the Church.[125]

The invitation by the Congregation suggests two things that will "offer better service to Christ and his brothers": entrustment to Mary and Eucharistic adoration. The word *better* indicates that we need to do more in this area because there is an increasing

---

[125] Cláudio Cardinal Hummes, Letter to Bishops, December 8, 2007, emphasis added.

need for interior renewal of priests for growth in sanctification. Interior renewal is closely connected with inner healing.

Fr. Cantalamessa beautifully writes about the healing power of "Eucharistic contemplation":

> Eucharistic contemplation also has an extraordinary power of healing. In the desert God ordered Moses to raise a bronze serpent on a pole. All those who were bitten by poisonous snakes and then looked at the bronze serpent were healed (cf. Numbers 21:4-9). Jesus applied the mysterious symbol of the bronze serpent to himself (John 3:14). What we should do, then, when afflicted by the venomous bites of pride, sensuality, and all the other illnesses of the soul is not to get lost in vain considerations or seek excuses, but to run before the Most Blessed Sacrament, to look at the Host and let healing pass through the same organ through which evil so often passes: our eyes.
>
> The only thing the Holy Spirit asks of us is that we give him our time, even if at the beginning it might seem like lost time. I will never forget the lesson that was given to me one day in this regard. I said to God, "Lord, give me fervor and I will give you all the time you desire in prayer." I found the answer in my heart: "Raniero, give me your time and I will give you all the fervor you want in prayer."[126]

This is a message for our time because this type of healing is sorely needed. Our eyes are meant to behold what is holy, good, true, and beautiful. Unfortunately, our eyes are bombarded by worldly things that are unholy, false, and ugly. Gazing upon the

---

[126] *This Is My Body*, 33.

face of Jesus and contemplating His beauty, purity, and goodness is the healing balm we need to be renewed.

Jesus awaits us in every tabernacle of the world where the glow of the sanctuary lamp invites us to come and *be* with the One who has proven His love for us. His life, death, and Resurrection are proofs of His love. Further proof of the extravagance of His love for humanity are the sacraments, of which the Eucharist is the crown jewel.

Although we may have good intentions, we often fail to pray or visit Jesus in the Blessed Sacrament because our daily lives are too busy. It is countercultural to come apart simply to *be* with the Lord. Learning how to *rest in God* is a gift of prayer called *contemplation*.[127] Contemplative prayer leads to a deep, abiding encounter with God. Fr. Cantalamessa writes, "Contemplation is an eminently personal activity; it calls for silence and requires that one be isolated from everything and everyone to concentrate on the object contemplated and to be lost in it."[128]

Through the gift of faith, we discover the *Divine Somebody* whose love is incomprehensible, extravagant, healing, and infinitely perfect. No one can encounter Jesus and remain the same, because an experience of divine love changes everything. An authentic encounter with Jesus in the silence of prayer leads to conversion of heart. Constancy in prayer leads to perpetual conversion; absent prayer, conversion will cease. Through an authentic encounter with Jesus, we change from within — we turn toward God and away from what is not of God. The process

---

[127] *Contemplation* derives from the Latin word *contemplatio*, which means "rest." In contemplative prayer, we rest in God's love and let grace work in us.

[128] *This Is My Body*, 25.

of encounter and conversion leads to engagement with Jesus in a deep personal relationship of mutual love and friendship.

There is a progression:

- *Encounter* with Jesus: personal experience in silence/contemplation;

- *Conversion* of heart: movement toward God and away from what is not of God;

- *Engagement* with Jesus in a relationship of love that leads to service.

Here, I am reminded of the famous words of Bl. Mother Teresa of Calcutta:

> *The fruit of silence is prayer.*
> *The fruit of prayer is faith.*
> *The fruit of faith is love.*
> *The fruit of love is service.*
> *The fruit of service is peace.*[129]

An encounter with divine love is a meeting with Jesus, who laid down His life to save you and me—it must become personal! It is personal to Christ, who hung from the Cross and desires souls *to satisfy His perpetual thirst.* Jesus is always present for us on the altars of His Church, in the tabernacles of the world. He awaits us there, but He also initiates an encounter with us. What's more, He also goes out after us— He pursues us to the ends of the earth, seeking after the human family like the Good Shepherd who left the ninety-nine sheep to search

---

[129] Quoted in Fr. Brian Kolodiejchuk, M.C., *Where There Is Love, There Is God: A Path to Closer Union with God and Greater Love for Others* (New York: Image, 2012), 16.

for the one lost lamb. No matter where we may run or hide, He is there—inviting us to an encounter of love. This is the most touching thing to me. It is not that we have loved Him but that He has loved us first (cf. 1 John 4:10).

Francis Thompson's famous poem "The Hound of Heaven" is published in the Liturgy of the Hours.[130] It portrays a God who persistently pursues each person, hoping for a *saving encounter*. It begins with the story of flight from God, proceeds to tell how God pursues, and ends with the longed-for encounter of truth and love. The first stanza tells of his flight from God:

> *I fled Him, down the nights and down the days;*
> *I fled Him, down the arches of the years;*
> *I fled Him, down the labyrinthine ways*
> *Of my own mind; and in the midst of tears*
> *I hid from Him, and under running laughter.*[131]

The second-to-last stanza tells of God's embrace and their encounter:

> *"Strange, piteous, futile thing!*
> *Wherefore should any set thee love apart?*
> *Seeing none but I makes much of naught" (He said),*
> *"And human love needs human meriting:*
> *How hast thou merited—*
> *Of all man's clotted clay the dingiest clot?*

[130] The Liturgy of the Hours is the official daily public prayer of the Church, is obligatory for priests and religious, and is optional for lay people.

[131] International Commission on English in the Liturgy, Inc., *The Liturgy of the Hours*, Vol. 3 (New York: Catholic Book Publishing Co., 1975), 1989.

Alack, thou knowest not
How little worthy of any love thou art!
Whom wilt thou find to love ignoble thee,
Save Me, save only Me?
All which I took from thee I did but take,
Not for thy harms,
But just that thou might'st seek it in My arms.
All which thy child's mistake
Fancies as lost, I have stored for thee at home:
Rise, clasp My hand, and come!"[132]

Jesus is the stupendous Divine Lover who always does amazing things in pursuit of His people. During my daily Holy Hour, I often gaze at the hidden God in the Sacred Host in awe of the humility of Jesus, who condescends to become so little and vulnerable to His creatures. I beg my Lord to make me humble, to crucify my pride, which hides itself in so many clever ways unknown to me. What a relief it is for me to come before Jesus without pretense. It is refreshing to be utterly transparent before God. Many times He has allowed me to see myself in the light of truth, and I repeat the words of Peter, "Depart from me, Lord, for I am a sinner" (cf. Luke 5:8). Then I am filled with blessed assuredness of divine mercy that absorbs my forgiven sins. Jesus is merciful even in His discipline of the soul. He draws us to His Sacred Heart, where the fire of divine love burns away the dross of our fallen nature. Then slowly but surely we are purified in the embers of divine love.

Jesus the Eternal High Priest remains with us so that we may have abundant life on earth and eternal life in heaven. God

[132] Ibid., 1992-1993.

knows how desperate we are to encounter him. He knows that without the encounter of divine love, we languish amid many counterfeit loves.

Recall the encounter between Jesus and Zacchaeus (Luke 19:1-10). Zacchaeus, a crooked tax collector, short in stature, climbed a tree so that he could see Jesus passing by. He was probably just curious. But Jesus noticed him and called him by name to come down from the tree because He wanted to go to his house. Jesus knew Zacchaeus needed to encounter the truth that would set him free. Because of that merciful encounter with Jesus, salvation came to the house of Zacchaeus, a sinner. Jesus initiated the encounter with Zacchaeus that day. In our day, Jesus continues to initiate the encounter because He is present and waiting in every tabernacle of the world. Jesus has already shown up; He waits for us to show up too.

When we come to worship and adore Jesus in the Blessed Sacrament, we must come as we are—sinners in need of a Savior. We can anticipate an encounter with Jesus and the experience of divine love enfolding us. We may not feel the experience emotionally, but we will discover the existence of divine love animating us through life in moments of joy and sorrow, in consolation and desolation.

Offering a Holy Hour for Priests

When I offer a Holy Hour for priests, I invoke the Holy Spirit to lead me in praying for the priest in greatest need of help. I reflect on the encounter between Jesus and Bartimaeus (Mark 10:46-52), in which Jesus asks, "What do you want me to do for you?" Bartimaeus replies, "I want to see." In my time with Jesus, I want to see how to help a priest in need of prayer.

Praying for Priests

There are many priests who desire to see:

- themselves as they really are;
- God and His presence in their lives;
- the true path of sanctity they are called to walk, the narrow and steep Way of the Cross;
- their way through a culture that is largely anti-clerical, anti-Church, and anti-God;
- how to live out a priesthood animated by the zeal of their first vocational encounter with Jesus;
- the glory of God in and through their priesthood.

I believe that Jesus wants to lead us in prayer, for He takes no delight in spiritual blindness or deadness. He desires for us to come out of the tombs we hide in — into the light of the Holy of Holies so that we might pray to the Father, commune with heaven, and receive strength and wisdom for the journey.

Once during a Holy Hour for priests, I asked God to show me how to pray for priests. Within the silence of my heart I heard the still, small voice of God:

Pray for the priests who are in spiritual desolation due to a lack of prayer and penance. Invoke the Holy Spirit to breathe on the dry bones of some of my priests. Pray for priests who do not pray. Some forsake their priestly duty to pray the Divine Office. Some pray superficially and deprive themselves of divine intimacy. Pray for the priests who identify with the spirit of the world instead of the Cross of salvation. I receive your prayers for those priests who cannot or will not pray at this time. I will renew and sanctify them — for behold, I make all things new.

The Holy Hour: An Encounter with Jesus

About a year later, I read a book entitled *To My Priests*, which records the Lord's words to Ven. Conchita. The prophetic words she received more than eighty years ago seem very similar to Jesus's present request for continued prayer for priests:

> I want to rebuild the sunken hearts of many of my priests; I want to wake up their slumbering souls; I want to move the loving fibers in the very depths of priestly hearts that they might respond to my longing to perfect them in unity; I want my protests to penetrate their sentiments sickened by contact with a world that has distanced them from me.
>
> I want to bring them into my arms, press them to my heart, and impart fire, light, love, life! I confide to you that my heart full of tenderness and charity deeply desires all of this.
>
> I promise that this heavenly impulse for my priests will not remain unfulfilled; it will make itself felt at a future time throughout the world.[133]

On another occasion, during a time of adoration following Holy Thursday Mass (celebrating the institution of the Eucharist and the priesthood), Jesus spoke silently in my heart of His tremendous love for His brother priests. I wrote in my private prayer journal:

> I saw them all that night in the Upper Room—each unique brother of mine who would share the cup of royalty and become marked with the seal of sacramental

---

[133] A Mis Sacerdotes, 306-307, 308 (text translated by John Nahrgang).

117

priesthood. I saw their goodness, intent on doing as I told them. They listened intently to the Master, and I loved them as I love myself. I knew them and loved them with the most unfathomable divine charity! That night, the first Twelve were with me physically, but all men who would follow their footsteps were in my mind's eye and in my heart. I knew their future. I saw a brotherhood of heroic faith, hope, and love that would catch souls for the Kingdom. I knew also the future Judases — the few unfaithful brothers among all the faithful. I saw the troubles that would plague my priesthood down through the ages. I saw all those who would betray me and wound the Bride, the Church. I saw the many who would remain always faithful to me. I considered all human weakness and chose to perpetuate myself through these chosen men. I know my royal priesthood, the brothers of my heart — I know them and love them with all my divine love!

In light of sharing the words above, I propose some thoughts from a great theologian regarding the interior life: how we hear and listen to God's voice. Fr. Reginald Garrigou-Lagrange, O.P., wrote the spiritual classic *The Three Stages of the Interior Life*. This is one of the first books I read in my mid-thirties, when I was resuming a serious prayer life. It was through this priest's teachings that I felt comfortable opening my heart to interior conversation with God in the normal progression of the interior life. Fr. Garrigou-Lagrange teaches:

The interior life thus becomes more and more a conversation with God, in which man gradually frees himself from egoism, self-love, sensuality, and pride, in which, by frequent prayer, he asks the Lord for the ever-new graces he needs. His interior conversation changes so much that St. Paul can say, "Our conversation is in Heaven." St. Thomas often insisted on this point.

Therefore, the interior life is in a soul that is in the state of grace, especially in a life of humility, abnegation, faith, hope and charity with the peace given by the progressive subordination of our feelings and wishes to love God, who will be the object of our beatitude.

Hence, to have an interior life, an exceedingly active exterior apostolate does not suffice, nor does great theological knowledge; nor is the latter necessary. A generous beginner, who already has a genuine spirit of abnegation and prayer, already possesses a true interior life, which ought to continue developing.

Prayer takes the form of petition, of adoration, and thanksgiving; it is always an elevation of the soul toward God. And God answers by recalling to our minds what has been said to us in the Gospel, and what is useful for the sanctification of the present moment. Did not Christ say, "But the Paraclete, the Holy Spirit, whom the Father will send in my name, he will teach you all things and bring all things to your mind whatsoever I shall have said to you" (John 14:26)?[134]

Continuing the theme of encountering the Eternal High Priest during the Holy Hour, I now share a personal testimony that illustrates the amazing grace that occurs in prayer before the Blessed Sacrament.

---

[134] Fr. Reginald Garrigou-Lagrange, O.P., *The Three Ages of the Interior Life*, vol. 1 (Rockford, IL: TAN Books, 1989), 46.

Praying for Priests

Holy Hour: Encountering Divine Mercy

With Mary, my soul magnifies the Lord, who has blessed me in countless ways beyond what is shared here. Through many dark days and nights, Jesus the Eternal High Priest carried me through tumultuous waters. My encounters with Jesus during daily Holy Hours undoubtedly saved my family as the cross bore down upon us.

Regrettably, the practice of my faith was mediocre at best during the first seven years of my marriage because my eyes were fixed on financial success and not on God. My husband and I worked very hard and at the age of thirty, we moved into an exclusive neighborhood. I worked in medical office management until the birth of our second son and then stayed home to raise the children and focus on the family.

When our sons entered Catholic grammar school, one of the school mothers invited me to attend a weekly Rosary prayer group. I had to relearn the prayers, but when I resumed praying our Lady's Rosary, my heart became convicted that I had offended God by allowing worldliness to eclipse my relationship with Him.

As I prayed the Rosary regularly and witnessed the faith of the prayer group, I began to experience a conversion of heart. A year later, my conversion was solidified during a pilgrimage to Lourdes, where I experienced Mary leading me into an encounter with the Real Presence of her Son. I spoke to the pilgrimage priest adviser regarding some prayer experiences at Lourdes and other holy sites in France where we had prayed. He offered to become my spiritual director. I returned from the pilgrimage and happily resumed family life while continuing to abide with Christ in prayer. I began attending daily Mass with renewed fervor.

The Holy Hour: An Encounter with Jesus

During my first spiritual-direction meeting, I was encouraged to begin the practice of a daily Holy Hour.

At that time, my family seemingly had no problems at all. My daily Holy Hour cultivated a love of silence, and my relationship with the Lord grew quickly. I began to distinguish the still, small voice of Jesus in my heart, whispering sentiments of love and inviting me to pray for His intentions for the Church, for priests, and for the salvation of souls. I emerged from my Holy Hours more peaceful and joyful as these encounters with Jesus enkindled the fire of divine love within me. This helped me to become a better wife and mother through my growth in patience, kindness, and inner peace.

Around the same time, some women in the prayer group invited me to help start a Magnificat chapter in our diocese. I wasn't very interested since I was a busy mother of two young sons with a husband developing his own business. Eventually, the daily Holy Hour gave me courage to accept the invitation. Twenty-three years later, I'm still privileged to serve in the leadership of this ministry, which has grown to become an international apostolate with widespread ecclesial support.

All was well until one beautiful spring Saturday morning. As we were on our way to watch our sons play in their Little League baseball games, we received a phone call asking us to come immediately to the local hospital, where my father-in-law had just been admitted. Two women driving by had seen him lying in a pool of blood on the sidewalk in front of our family lumber business and called the paramedics.

We arrived at the hospital and were shocked to see that our beloved father had been severely beaten about the head by a large timber. The damage to his face and head were so severe that he was unrecognizable; there was no semblance of his former wonderful countenance! The surgeons attempted to save his life by performing a frontal lobectomy. After we waited and prayed for a few hours, the doctors wheeled him out of the operating room and advised our family that he would be able to survive for only about another hour by artificial means, just enough time for the rest of the family to say their goodbyes. In grief and anticipation, we hovered around this beloved father of six, the glue of our families, a bright light of love, Irish wit, and German strength. After a few hours, he breathed his last as our inconsolable family cried gut-wrenching tears of the deepest anguish, shock, and grief.

Although the case aired on *America's Most Wanted*, the two robbers who killed our father were never found.

It is impossible to describe the effect of such trauma on our family, especially my husband, who had worked closely with his dad in the family business. Our former innocence was lost, and our life would never be the same. I felt acutely the horror of absolute disrespect for human life. During the funeral Mass, the Lord reminded me of the culture of death, wherein license is given for a woman to abort her child, which in turn erodes our culture's appreciation of the sanctity of life.

After the funeral, our family tried to carry on, to help our mother with the loss of her husband, and to keep the business moving forward. Many in the family simply shut down emotionally, and a veil of silence descended over the horror of the murder. But I could not contain my agony. Tears flowed spontaneously whenever I was alone. Perhaps I was mourning for those who would not allow themselves to mourn.

Daily I ran to Jesus in the Blessed Sacrament and remained there conversing with Him, often for hours. Oh, how I protested to God for allowing this to happen! I had no peace of soul, only the anguish of trying to comprehend what had happened to our happy life! Anger welled up within me. After a few weeks of struggling back and forth with Jesus in the tabernacle, I heard His gentle voice in my heart: *Please pray for the murderers.*

Oh, how indignant I became! I refused my Lord's request repeatedly. Yet I was drawn like a magnet to the tabernacle every day, where I received strength not to weep in front of my husband, my children, and my mother-in-law. Jesus continued to ask me to pray for the murderers, and I continued to resist. Then one day He really got my attention when I heard these words in my heart: *I am only asking that you repeat the words I said from the Cross: "Father, forgive them; for they not know what they do"* (Luke 23:34).

I decided that I would try to echo the Lord's words, although I still felt emotions quite contrary to forgiveness. During my Holy Hours, I kept repeating His words of mercy. My tears ceased, my anger quelled, my peace returned, and my joy came back. Eventually, I could pray the words of forgiveness from my heart.

During my Holy Hours, Jesus flooded my soul with the realization of how much He loves everyone, even the sinner and the murderer. I became overwhelmed with an awareness of His infinite divine mercy. He then invited me actually to become *a vessel of divine mercy* not only for the murderers, but also for others.

Jesus desires all to be saved, and that is why He remains with us always in the Sacrament of the Altar, in His Body, Blood, Soul, and Divinity. My daily Holy Hours became healing encounters with the Divine Physician. Divine mercy became the medicine to quell the terror of the trauma that shook my family.

Praying for Priests

We Wish to See Jesus

Pope John Paul II once reflected upon these words from the Gospel: "We wish to see Jesus" (John 12:21).

> This request, addressed to the Apostle Philip by some Greeks who had made a pilgrimage to Jerusalem for the Passover, echoes spiritually in our ears. Like those pilgrims of two thousand years ago, the men and women of our own day — often unconsciously — ask believers not only to *speak* of Christ, but in a certain sense to *show* him to them. And the Church's task is to reflect the light of Christ in every historical period, and to make his face shine before generations. Our witness, however, would be hopelessly inadequate if we ourselves had not first *contemplated his face*.[135]

Recall the biblical encounters of Peter with the Eternal High Priest at the various stages of his journey — the initial *yes* of Peter to follow Jesus, his eventual *denial* of Jesus, and then the *encounters* with Jesus, first on the day of His Resurrection, then on the shore of Galilee when the risen Lord reinstated Peter by asking him three times if he loved Him, received three yeses, and then asked him to feed his sheep (John 21:15-17).

These Petrine encounters reveal God's mercy for an ordinary chosen man upon whom He built His Church. Peter is changed incrementally, as most of us are. His encounters with Christ strengthened him on the path to his own crucifixion for the sake of love. Peter said yes quickly, then fell to temptation quickly, but

---

[135] John Paul II, *Novo Millennio Ineunte*, no. 16.

picked himself up and began again to fulfill his unique mission as the first Vicar of Christ.

We should not deprive ourselves of a daily encounter with Jesus. Furthermore, through the Church, He invites us now to bring our intercessory prayer to the tabernacle to pray for the sanctification of priests and for vocations.

Why do we need to carry all priests to the tabernacle? Ven. Archbishop Sheen reveals the reason:

> Supplication, mediation and pleading have always been heard by God. Wrath would have been visited on the Jewish people had not Moses interceded (Exodus 32:9-14, Deuteronomy 9:18, 20, 25-28). Job interceded for the three counseling specialists who gave him wrong answers (Job 42:8-10). Even in marriage: "For the heathen husband now belongs to God through his Christian wife and the heathen wife through her Christian husband" (1 Corinthians 7:14). There is no reason to suppose that this would not apply to cities or nations if there were sufficiently holy priests, as Sodom and Gomorrah would have been saved for ten just men.
>
> In medicine, when a patient is suffering from anemia, blood will be transferred from a healthy person to cure the sick of that condition. Skin is grafted from the back to the face to repair a burn. If blood can be transfused and skin grafted, then prayers and sacrifices can be transmitted to the sick members of the Mystical Body of Christ. The motivation for a Holy Hour is reparation. We pray for those who do not pray, we make acts of faith in the Real Presence for those who lack or who have lost the faith. In a word, we are their victims,

like Christ, innocent but one with their guilt in the progressive redemption of mankind. The Holy Hour in our modern rat race is necessary for authentic prayer.[136]

Jesus, Eternal High Priest,
graciously draw us into an abiding
encounter of divine love through
Your Eucharistic Presence.
In the glow of the sanctuary lamp,
let us meet You in expectant faith.
In silent contemplation, let us
receive Your holy instruction.

Attract us in prayer and give us
an abiding desire to live in accord
with Your Eucharistic Heart.

Convert our hearts,
heal our wounds, and empower
us to bear witness to others,
that we might fulfill this
mission of prayer for priests
for the New Evangelization.

---

[136] *Those Mysterious Priests*, 187.

6

⚜

The Holy Rosary: A School of Prayer

The Rosary, reclaimed in its full meaning, goes to the very heart of Christian life; it offers a familiar yet fruitful spiritual and educational opportunity for personal contemplation, the formation of the People of God, and the new evangelization.[137]
—St. John Paul II

I have anchored this book, in part, in the scriptural Rosary because the Congregation for the Clergy, taking inspiration from St. John Paul II, strongly encourages praying the Rosary for priests, especially in the exalted atmosphere of adoration before the Blessed Sacrament. In the 2012 edition of the Congregation's booklet, then Cardinal Mauro Piacenza quotes Pope John Paul II in his 2004 Apostolic Letter for the Year of the Eucharist:

> Let us deepen through adoration our personal and communal contemplation, drawing upon aids to prayer inspired by the word of God and the experience of so many mystics, old and new. The Rosary itself, when it is profoundly

[137] *Rosarium Virginis Mariae*, no. 3

understood in the biblical and Christocentric form ...
will prove a particularly fitting introduction to Eucharistic
contemplation, contemplation carried out with Mary as
our companion and guide.[138]

We see here that Eucharistic adoration of Jesus and the prayer
of the Rosary are complementary. The Rosary is principally composed of the prayer of Christ, the *Our Father*, and the Angelic
Salutation, the *Hail Mary*. In his 2002 apostolic letter *Rosarium
Virginis Mariae* (*On the Most Holy Rosary*), Pope John Paul II
develops this dynamic further:

> The Rosary of the Virgin Mary, which gradually took form
> in the second millennium under the guidance of the Spirit
> of God, is a prayer loved by countless saints and encour-
> aged by the Magisterium. Simple yet profound, it still
> remains, at the dawn of this third millennium, a prayer
> of great significance destined to bring forth a harvest of
> holiness. It blends easily into the spiritual journey of the
> Christian life, which, after two thousand years, has lost
> none of the freshness of its beginning and feels drawn by
> the Spirit of God to "set out into the deep" (*duc in altum!*)
> in order once more to proclaim, and even cry out, before
> the world that Jesus Christ is Lord and Savior, "the way,
> and the truth and the life" (Jn 14:6), "the goal of human
> history and the point on which the desires of history and
> civilization turn."

The Rosary, though clearly Marian in character, is
at heart a Christocentric prayer. In the sobriety of its

---

[138] *Eucharistic Adoration for the Sanctification of Priests and Spiritual
Maternity*, 44.

elements, it has all the *depth of the Gospel message in its entirety*, of which it can be said to be a compendium. It is an echo of the prayer of Mary, her perennial *Magnificat* for the work of redemptive Incarnation, which began in her virginal womb. With the Rosary, the Christian people *sits at the school of Mary* and is led to contemplate the beauty of the face of Christ and to experience the depths of his love. Through the Rosary, the faithful receive abundant grace, as though from the very hands of the Mother of the Redeemer.[139]

I ardently testify that the Rosary is a spiritual powerhouse of prayer. Twenty-three years ago, I had a profound conversion of heart through the Rosary, a return to the practice of the Faith after seven years of spiritual mediocrity with little or no prayer. When I took up praying the Rosary, it unlocked my mind and heart to an authentic experience of Jesus. The Rosary was an instrument of inner healing that helped reorient my mind to Christ so that I could leave behind the worldliness I had chosen for a time. When I began praying the Rosary daily for serious family situations, the fruit was miraculous in every case. There is not enough room in this book to share all the miraculous stories that came to my family through the Rosary! Never did the Rosary fail as intercessory prayer for my family as we went through a long period of intense suffering. Sometimes it would take a year of praying the Rosary for a particular intention, but in the end the grace would come for every trial.

Through the Rosary, peace and courage enabled me to carry my cross not with bitterness but with abandonment to God. I

---

[139] *Rosarium Virginis Mariae*, no. 1.

learned to trust that God will bring great good out of every suffering that is united to His Passion. The greatest solace came when I contemplated the Sorrowful Mysteries of the Rosary before the Blessed Sacrament. I would see that my suffering, seemingly so great, was actually small in comparison with the Lord's Passion. I was not crushed but transformed by suffering. Mary taught me to keep my eyes on Christ by meditating on the mysteries of the Rosary, pondering the Lord's life, death, and Resurrection.

In 1917, Our Lady of Fátima made a plea: "Say the Rosary every day, to obtain peace for the world."[140] When the Berlin Wall fell in 1989, I remember my wise father-in-law being delighted but not surprised by the news; he had said that the event was the result of the prayers of a generation of people who had suffered war but had taken to heart the message of Our Lady of Fátima and committed themselves to praying the Rosary for the sake of peace. I was inspired by his matter-of-fact confidence in Our Lady of Fátima 's message.

Pope John Paul II was often seen and pictured with a rosary in his hand. I wonder how many thousands of rosaries he gave to the faithful who came to his papal audiences. I know many people who cherish the rosary he gave to them! The Polish pope spoke from the heart about the impact of the Rosary on him and on his pontificate:

> I myself have often encouraged the frequent recitation of the Rosary. From my youthful years this prayer has held an important place in my spiritual life. I was powerfully reminded of this during my recent visit to Poland, and in particular at the Shrine of Kalwaria. The Rosary has

---

[140] Quoted in John D. Miller, *Beads and Prayers: The Rosary in History and Devotion* (London: Burns & Oates, 2002), 158.

accompanied me in moments of joy and in moments of difficulty. To it I have entrusted any number of concerns; in it I have always found comfort. Twenty-four years ago, 29 October 1978, scarcely two weeks after my election to the See of Peter, I frankly admitted: "The Rosary is my favorite prayer. A marvelous prayer! Marvelous in its simplicity and its depth!... Against the background of the words *Ave Maria* the principal events of the life of Jesus Christ pass before the eyes of the soul. They take shape in the complete series of the joyful, sorrowful, and glorious mysteries, and they put us in living communion with Jesus through—we might say—the heart of his Mother. At the same time our hearts can embrace in the decades of the Rosary all the events that make up the lives of individuals, families, nations, the Church, and all mankind; our personal concerns and those of our neighbor, especially those who are closest to us, who are dearest to us. Thus the simple prayers of the Rosary mark the rhythm of human life."

... How many graces have I received in these from the Blessed Virgin through the Rosary: *Magnificat anima mea Dominum!* I wish to lift up my thanks to the Lord in the words of his Most Holy Mother, under whose protection I have placed my Petrine ministry: *Totus Tuus!*[141]

Pope John Paul II's devotion to the Rosary was deep and influential and in 2005 was personally witnessed in a powerful way by none other than Cardinal Jorge Mario Bergoglio, whom we know today as Pope Francis:

---

[141] *Rosarium Virginis Mariae*, no. 2.

If I remember well it was 1985. One evening I went to recite the holy Rosary that was being led by the Holy Father. He was in front of everybody, on his knees. The group was numerous; I saw the Holy Father from the back and, little by little, I got lost in prayer. I was not alone: I was praying in the middle of the people of God to which I and all those there belonged, led by our Pastor.

In the middle of the prayer I became distracted, looking at the figure of the Pope: his pity, his devotion was a witness. And the time drifted away, and I began to imagine the young priest, the seminarian, the poet, the worker, the child from Wadowice ... in the same position in which knelt at that moment, reciting *Ave Maria* after *Ave Maria*. His witness struck me. I felt that this man, chosen to lead the Church, was following a path up to his Mother in the sky, a path set out on from his childhood. And I became aware of the density of the words of the Mother of Guadalupe to St. Juan Diego: "Don't be afraid, am I not perhaps your mother?" I understood the presence of Mary in the life of the Pope.

That testimony did not get forgotten in an instant. From that time on I have recited the fifteen mysteries of the Rosary every day.[142]

In November of 2013, Catholic News Service published a charming article describing how Pope Francis gave away twenty thousand boxes, each containing a rosary, a Divine Mercy holy card, and what looked like instructions for taking a prescription,

---

[142] "The Remembrances of Twenty Cardinals," *30 Days* 4 (2005), accessed December 3, 2013, http://www.30giorni.it/articoli_ id_8513_13.htm.

to a large gathering of pilgrims in St. Peter's Square. At the conclusion of his Sunday *Angelus* address, he told the crowd, "I want to recommend some medicine for all of you. It's a spiritual medicine." He held up a medicine box with a human heart imprinted on it and informed the pilgrims that there was a rosary in each box. He added, "Don't forget to take it. It's good for your heart, for your soul, for your whole life."

The article went on to explain that the directions-for-use sheet that came with the boxes recommended "daily use of the beads for both adults and children … that receiving the sacraments increases the efficacy of the prescription and that further information and assistance can be received from any priest."[143]

I couldn't help but note that this holy remedy offered by Pope Francis contrasts greatly with a disturbing and devastating trend I have witnessed in healing and deliverance ministry: a rapid increase in addiction to prescription medicine. I'm convinced that the best medicine for what ails the human family today is *precisely* what Pope Francis has prescribed—a daily dose of the Rosary and the Chaplet of Divine Mercy. If people take this spiritual medicine, they will end up in the confessional and at the table of the Lord, and I'm convinced that the evil one's power to oppress the people of God will be weakened.

I have often said that I have a big addiction to praying the Rosary because it has become a holy habit in my life. I pray it everywhere possible: on my daily walk, in my car, during Holy Hours, on planes, at coffee shops, in my prayer room at home,

---

[143] Cindy Wooden, "Pope Prescribes Daily Rosary for What Ails You," Catholic News Service, November 18, 2013, accessed December 1, 2013, http://www.catholicnews.com/data/stories/cns/1304848.htm.

and on the phone with priests and seminarians. However, after ten years of attending daily Mass and Holy Hour and praying the Rosary several times a day, I gave in to the temptation that I could take a break from such an intense spiritual regimen. I succumbed to the temptation to "relax a little" and thought I could do so without serious consequences. Within two weeks, I realized I was losing my faith quickly! Other things had eclipsed God out of my mind and heart. My close relationship with Jesus waned, while worldly things distracted me.

Then I went to confession to repent of my presumption, laziness, stupidity, and pride! Afterward, I booked five days at a local monastery to enter into a schedule of prayer and contemplation. I have never again deliberately gone down that slippery slope again.

This experience reminds me of the body's need for physical exercise. Even if we've been disciplined about physical exercise for years, if we stop exercising, the muscles of our body atrophy quickly. The discipline of prayer is necessary, and in my experience, the most efficacious prayer outside of the Mass and Holy Hour is the Rosary. It's simple but profound.

The Rosary is a *contemplative* prayer and an *intercessory* prayer. It is also a *weapon* against the evil one. I have witnessed this as part of a team helping priests in official rites of exorcism. The devil and his legions are real, and they detest Mary and her holy Rosary! Once, during intense deliverance prayers by our priest leader, the demon screamed through the mouth of the poor victim, "Stop saying those beads! Those beads burn me!" Unbeknownst to the victim, her mother was in an upstairs room praying continuous Rosaries for her daughter. In my experience of assisting at exorcisms, the Rosary has been continuously prayed, either silently or aloud. The *Catechism* asserts that prayer is a battle and that man's entire life is a battle against the evil one (nos. 409, 2725). God made a provision for this by equipping the Church with an arsenal of spiritual power (the sacraments and sacramentals) to make us victorious over evil. The Rosary is one of the primary weapons of prayer. I observed that demons react most powerfully against the words of Scripture and anything having to do with Mary. The Rosary is both a Marian prayer and a scriptural prayer, so it is a weapon that does tremendous damage to the demonic world.

Personal Testimony: The Rosary's Power
to Intercede for Persecutors

To testify to the intercessory power of the Rosary and the importance of praying for persecutors, and to encourage wider use of this weapon of prayer, I would like to share with you a family experience.

My younger brother, to whom I am very close in age and affinity, is a well-known transplant surgeon. He was the director of a successful transplant program at a big hospital and is also married to a medical doctor. Their lives are devoted to saving lives.

On one occasion, there was a mix-up involving an organ transplant that was given to the wrong patient. My brother was not the operating surgeon, nor was he even in the hospital on the night of the surgery. Rather, he was with his young wife, who had just been diagnosed with breast cancer. One of his on-call colleagues performed the transplant. Multiple personnel at the hospital altered medical records in a cover-up that was later discovered through an audit. Since my brother was the director of the transplant program, he was indicted for both the misappropriation of the organ transplant and the cover-up. The FBI charged him with eight felonies. If proven guilty, he would have served 120 years in prison. The case developed over eight years before he finally had his day in court, and it was an eight-year nightmare for our entire family. It especially took its toll on his two young sons, not to mention our aging parents.

I will never forget the first day at federal court when I walked into that courtroom with my rosary in hand to sit next to my brother's wife in the front row. A faithful priest-friend of the family also sat with us to pray. There were also many FBI attorneys and personnel present.

There sat my brave brother with his one attorney. He looked so small; it seemed as if all odds were against him. He had been offered some plea bargains beforehand and had refused, insisting on his innocence. I admit to thinking, when I saw the Goliath opposition he faced, that he should have pleaded to a lesser charge. As the prosecutor began the tedious questioning of witnesses, I noted the humble jury of ordinary men and women: schoolteachers, bus drivers, and the like. Having worked in a medical surgical office for many years, I wondered how they would equitably assess the medical and legal terminology of the case. I began to cry out to the Lord for help. I begged the Lord to show me how to pray for the situation. I wanted to condemn the prosecutors who were spewing false accusations against my brother.

The Holy Spirit began to give me an inspiring certitude about how to pray, prompting me to intercede *for the judge, the jury, and the team of prosecutors!* The Lord prompted me to pray for a spirit of truth to descend upon the courtroom, a spirit of wisdom to descend upon the jury, a spirit of humility to descend upon the prosecutors, and a spirit of clarity to descend upon the judge. The Lord inspired me to call upon St. Michael the Archangel to escort any and all spirits that were not of God away from the courtroom. Amazing things began to happen when I prayed in this manner, offering up one decade of the Rosary for particular persons. For example, a juryman raised his hand, and the judge interrupted the prosecutor to ask what the problem was. The juror replied that the prosecutor's witness was receiving hand signals from an attorney in the back of the room! The judge threw the attorney out. Several other things happened that induced a dramatic shift in the atmosphere in favor of my brother.

After a week of the prosecution making its case, my brother's attorney decided to rest the case without a defense! My brother would not take the stand, nor would one witness for the defense. My brother's attorney was that confident of winning the case! I wasn't so sure. Interesting also is that my brother was silent for eight years, refusing media interviews and the opportunity to defend himself. He hoped to do so in a court of law, but now he was asked to remain silent in his own defense. God was inviting blind trust.

The day arrived when the verdict would be decided. My sister-in-law and I walked to the cathedral down the street from the federal court building to attend noon Mass. As the Mass began, the jury also began their deliberations.

The readings, the Gospel, and the homily all spoke about vindication, but I was afraid to believe that God was speaking to me through the liturgy, as He often does! After Mass—the greatest intercessory prayer of all—we returned to the courtroom and waited. At about 3:00 p.m. on Friday afternoon, the hour of Divine Mercy, the jury returned, and we held our breath while all eight counts were read aloud by the judge. The countdown began. Count one—not guilty. Count two—not guilty. Count three—not guilty. And so it went all the way to count eight—not guilty! When I hugged my brother, he tearfully whispered to me,

"Our prayers have been answered!" I was overwhelmed by God's fidelity and power in a situation that seemed doomed to defeat and disaster. God is almighty! Prayer moves mountains!

Members of the jury came to embrace us afterward, saying, "We saw that they set you up as a scapegoat from the first moment!" I realized then that the common sense of ordinary people is sufficient for justice.

A few nights following my brother's acquittal, he was called in to the hospital emergency room because a young woman had been stabbed while walking home from work and was in critical condition. The first surgical team had operated on her but failed to repair a vital organ, and she was in danger of dying. They needed a liver surgeon in order to save her life. My brother operated on the young woman and saved her life. He called me and said, "Sis, God works in mysterious ways—he spared my life [in prison] so I could spare this girl's life."

Let us never underestimate the power of intercessory prayer! God is the God of miracles. If only we had faith the size of a mustard seed, we'd expect the greater works of God to be realized in our midst. Thanks be to God and to His Mother, whose heel indeed steps on the head of the ancient serpent to protect her children.

The Scriptural Rosary: A Compendium of the Gospel

During one of the most trying times of raising my children, I learned firsthand the amazing efficacy of daily intercession for a child by praying the scriptural Rosary during Eucharistic adoration. It took one year for me to see the miraculous fruit of it, but when the grace of God came to my son, it was a life-changing and lasting miracle of liberation for which I still thank God. Using

St. Ignatius's method of meditation,[144] I would ask Mary to take my son mystically into the Gospel scene of each Rosary — directly into the life of Christ. This proved to be a very powerful method of intercession. Not only did my son benefit, but I also felt transported into scenes of the life of Christ.

Pope John Paul II beautifully explains how this dynamic is fruitful for us: "The cycles of meditation proposed by the holy Rosary are by no means exhaustive, but they do bring to mind what is essential and they awaken in a soul a thirst for a knowledge of Christ continually nourished by the pure source of the Gospel."[145]

The Congregation's 2012 booklet encourages the faithful to pray specifically *the scriptural Rosary for the sanctification of priests.* In *Rosarium Virginis Mariae*, John Paul II referred to the Rosary as a "compendium of the Gospel" and added the five Luminous Mysteries to the original fifteen mysteries of the Rosary:

> For the Rosary to become more fully a "compendium of the Gospel," it is fitting to add, following reflection on the Incarnation and the hidden life of Christ (*the joyful mysteries*) and before focusing on the sufferings of his Passion (*the sorrowful mysteries*) and triumph of his Resurrection (*the glorious mysteries*), a meditation on certain particularly significant moments in his public ministry (*the mysteries of light*). This addition of these new mysteries, without prejudice to any essential aspect of the prayer's traditional format, is meant to give it fresh life and to

---

[144] St. Ignatius of Loyola (1491-1556) was the founder of the Society of Jesus (Jesuits) and is regarded as one of the great masters of the spiritual life in the Catholic tradition.

[145] *Rosarium Virginis Mariae*, no. 24.

enkindle renewed interest in the Rosary's place within Christian spirituality as a true doorway to the depths of the Heart of Christ, ocean of joy and light, of suffering and of glory.[146]

In the next section, Pope John Paul II specifies the scriptural scenes corresponding to the mysteries of the Rosary. This further explains why the Rosary can be called a "compendium of the Gospel":

- *The Joyful Mysteries*: "The first five decades, the 'joyful mysteries,' are marked by *the joy radiating from the event of the Incarnation.* . . . To meditate upon the 'joyful' mysteries, then, is to enter into the ultimate causes and the deepest meaning of Christian joy."

- *The Mysteries of Light*: "In proposing to the Christian community five significant moments — 'luminous' mysteries — during this phase of Christ's life, I think that the following can be fittingly singled out: (1) his Baptism in the Jordan, (2) his self-manifestation at the wedding of Cana, (3) his proclamation of the Kingdom of God, with his call to conversion, (4) his Transfiguration, and finally, (5) his institution of the Eucharist, as the sacramental expression of the Paschal Mystery."

- *The Sorrowful Mysteries*: "The Gospels give great prominence to the sorrowful mysteries of Christ. . . . The Rosary selects certain moments from the Passion, inviting the faithful to contemplate them in their hearts and to relive them. . . . The sorrowful mysteries help

[146] *Rosarium Virginis Mariae*, no. 19.

the believer to relive the death of Jesus, to stand at the foot of the Cross beside Mary, to enter with her into the depths of God's love for man and to experience all its life-giving power."

♦ *The Glorious Mysteries*: "The contemplation of Christ's face cannot stop at the image of the Crucified One. He is the Risen One! The glorious mysteries ... lead the faithful to *greater hope for the eschatological*[147] *goal* toward which they journey as members of the pilgrim People of God in history. This can only impel them to bear courageous witness to that 'good news' which gives meaning to their entire existence."[148]

In this outline of the Rosary, we see that meditation on the mysteries of the Rosary is a Church-approved, time-tested way of plunging deeply into the Gospel. To contemplate the life of Christ with Mary is, for many Catholics, *the secret to deeper intimacy* with the Lord. Perhaps its miraculous effects should not surprise us, since it is based on the living Word of God, which is always effective, always alive, and always fruitful!

The Rosary Contains Mary's Memories

The prayer of the Rosary is a memorial of the life of Jesus. Each mystery of the Rosary is a mystery of remembrance of what God has done for His people. Pondering the life of Jesus Christ renews our minds and hearts and keeps us close to Him. Pondering His life with Mary intensifies our concentration on Him.

---

[147] The term *eschatological* refers to the "last things" (i.e., death, judgment, heaven, and hell).
[148] *Rosarium Virginis Mariae*, nos. 20, 21, 22, 23.

Pope John Paul II wrote that Mary remembers Christ in a "biblical sense," meaning that the memories do not only belong to history but *they are also part of the 'today' of salvation*."[149] In a sense, remembering *makes salvation history present* with its gift of grace. Remembering Jesus and what He has done for us (the Paschal mystery) is necessary for gratitude and a thriving faith.

This is also true of our personal history. For example, our extended family joined hands in prayer around our dinner table one recent Thanksgiving. Each person shared a reason for being grateful. After dinner, my eighty-year-old parents handed each of their five children an envelope containing many old photos taken of us as we were growing up in the fifties, sixties, and seventies. We spent hours together remembering occasions from our lives over the past fifty years. It was joyous to recall our family history and marvel at the passage of time and how we had grown! In recalling these episodes from our family life, our hearts were filled with awe and gratitude. We remembered how the grace of God carried us through the hills and valleys of the journey. And some moments represented in the pictures we not only remembered but somehow relived.

Mary remembers Christ and the history of salvation better than anyone else, since she accompanied her Son on His earthly pilgrimage. In *Rosarium Virginis Mariae*, Pope John Paul II writes about Mary's memories:

> Mary lived with her eyes fixed on Christ, treasuring his every word: "She kept all these things, pondering them in her heart" (Luke 2:19; cf. 2:51). The memories of Jesus, impressed upon her heart, were always with her, leading

[149] *Rosarium Virginis Mariae*, no. 13.

her to reflect on the various moments of her life at her Son's side. In a way those memories were to be the "rosary" which she recited uninterruptedly through her earthly life.

Even now, amid the joyful songs of the heavenly Jerusalem, the reasons for her thanksgiving and praise remain unchanged. They inspire her maternal concern for the pilgrim Church, in which she continues to relate her personal account of the Gospel. *Mary constantly sets before the faithful the "mysteries" of her Son*, with the desire that the contemplation of those mysteries will release all their saving power. In the recitation of the Rosary, the Christian community enters into contact with the memories and the contemplative gaze of Mary.[150]

When we pray Mary's Rosary, we walk with her, but she points us to Jesus. She teaches us to keep the memory of Christ alive within our hearts. Mary accompanied the Eternal High Priest in a way no other person did. That is why the Church looks to the Mother of the Eternal High Priest to help us understand the dignity and vocation of all priests so that we can grow to love them as she does, even to love them *with her maternal heart*. The praying of the Rosary helps us to open ourselves so that Mary can teach us to intercede for priests and vocations. Her maternal charity for priests can be *infused* into our hearts as we ponder the mysteries of Christ's life. She will help us fall in love with Jesus and His priests. Mary also keeps us mindful of the invaluable gift that the priest gives to the Church, the Eucharist.

I pray the Rosary *for* priests and seminarians, but I also pray the Rosary *with* priests and seminarians, in person and over the

[150] Ibid., no. 11.

phone. This has been one of the greatest joys of my life, because through it I have grown in my understanding of the interior disposition of the priestly heart. Recently while praying the Joyful Mysteries of the Rosary with my spiritual director, we both realized that this book and this new apostolate of prayer for priests has followed the way of the Joyful Mysteries!

When I pray the Rosary with priests, it is edifying to see the myriad of intentions they bring to prayer. The needs and concerns of all their parishioners, brother priests and bishops, their families, the Church, and the world are carried in their priestly hearts. While praying the Rosary, they offer these intentions to the Heart of Mary with trust in her maternal mediation. The priests I know truly inspire me to live Catholicism with ardent gratitude and joy. They are my heroes! Although they pass through trials and temptations, I see how grace always supplies for their needs.

Priests are brave men! The seminarians I have met are also extremely inspiring and very courageous. These men need and deserve the best of our intercessory prayers and sacrifices!

I once wrote a Rosary booklet as an intercessory tool for purity of body, mind, and spirit, and it has been a great joy for me to speak at seminaries about it. When I do so, I notice that many priests and seminarians pray the Rosary. I see them walking the seminary grounds with the beads passing through their fingers. What a glorious spiritual tool we have in the Rosary!

Praying the Scriptural Rosary for Priests

When I wrote my letter of proposal to the cardinal prefect of the Congregation for the Clergy, I asked for and received his blessing upon a large future number of prayer warriors to build up the Church through participation in a mission of intercessory prayer for priests and vocations as a part of the New Evangelization. In addition to the stories of spiritual mothers of priests featured in this book, there are present-day testimonies of priests, seminarians, and spiritual mothers on the website of the Foundation of Prayer for Priests.[151] It is my sincere hope that these stories will encourage others to participate in this vital mission. This is an urgent need of the Church, and it must be fulfilled for the salvation of souls. If we take the hand of Mary, she will lead us. Our prayers matter in the life of a priest, and the priest matters greatly in God's plan for humanity.

I strongly desire to inspire readers to intercede for priests and vocations in a special way through the scriptural Rosary; the following chapters of this book contain scriptural Rosaries for priests, vocations, and reparation. They draw in a special way from Holy Scripture and from two important documents written by Pope John Paul II. The Rosaries for priests and vocations both feature excerpts from *Pastores Dabo Vobis*, which, as I explained in chapter 2, provides key insights into the priestly character formed through the sacrament of Holy Orders and the importance of fruitful cooperation from all the people of God in supporting priests and vocations. The Rosary of reparation draws from *Salvifici Dolores*, a 1984 apostolic letter on the Christian meaning of human suffering.

I invite you to become a vessel of prayer for priests through the intercessory power of the Rosary. Please ask Mary (or Joseph) to give you her maternal (paternal) charity in praying Rosaries for priests. Mary and Joseph will help you to understand what God is asking of you. Consider how you can become a vessel of mercy, distributing prayer for the shepherds of the Church.

---

[151] Visit www.foundationforpriests.org.

Praying for Priests

We petition:

Mary, Queen of the Holy Rosary,
Mother of Priests and of the Church,
teach us to pray. Your Immaculate Heart is
a school of prayer. We place ourselves there
as your pupils. Pray that the Holy Spirit
will fill us with ardor for Jesus Christ
and zeal for the salvation of souls.
Write on our hearts God's Word
so that we may faithfully live out
the joyful, sorrowful, glorious and
luminous mysteries of our journey.
Help us go forth to proclaim
His marvelous deeds along the path
of the New Evangelization. Amen.

Part 2

⚜

Scriptural Rosaries
for the Mission

How to Pray the Scriptural Rosaries
in this Book

Sign of the Cross
Apostles' Creed
Our Father
Hail Mary (three times, for the
virtues of faith, hope, and charity)
Glory Be
Fátima Prayer

Announce the first mystery.
Read the Scripture passage,
the reflection, and the petition.
Our Father
Hail Mary (ten times while meditating
on the mystery for this decade)
Glory Be
Fátima Prayer
(Continue with the
remaining four mysteries.)

Hail, Holy Queen
Rosary Prayer

꘏

Prayers of the Rosary

Sign of the Cross
In the name of the Father, and of the Son, and of the Holy Spirit. Amen.

Apostles' Creed
I believe in God, the Father almighty, Creator of Heaven and earth, and in Jesus Christ, His only Son, our Lord, who was conceived by the Holy Spirit, born of the Virgin Mary, suffered under Pontius Pilate, was crucified, died, and was buried; He descended into hell; on the third day He rose again from the dead; He ascended into heaven and is seated at the right hand of God, the Father almighty; from there He will come to judge the living and the dead. I believe in the Holy Spirit, the holy Catholic Church, the communion of saints, the forgiveness of sins, the resurrection of the body, and life everlasting. Amen.

Our Father
Our Father, who art in heaven, hallowed be Thy name. Thy kingdom come. Thy will be done on earth as it is in heaven. Give us this day our daily bread, and forgive us

our trespasses, as we forgive those who trespass against us. And lead us not into temptation, but deliver us from evil. Amen.

Hail Mary

Hail Mary, full of grace, the Lord is with thee. Blessed art thou among women, and blessed is the fruit of thy womb, Jesus. Holy Mary, Mother of God, pray for us sinners, now and at the hour of our death. Amen.

Glory Be

Glory be to the Father, and to the Son, and to the Holy Spirit. As it was in the beginning is now, and ever shall be, world without end. Amen.

Fátima Prayer

O my Jesus, forgive us our sins, save us from the fires of hell, lead all souls to heaven, especially those in most need of Your mercy.

Hail, Holy Queen

Hail, holy Queen, mother of mercy, our life, our sweetness, and our hope. To thee do we cry, poor banished children of Eve. To thee do we send up our sighs, mourning, and weeping in this valley of tears. Turn then, most gracious advocate, thine eyes of mercy toward us, and after this our exile, show us the blessed fruit of thy womb, Jesus. O clement, O loving, O sweet Virgin Mary.

V. Pray for us, O Holy Mother of God.

R. That we may be made worthy of the promises of Christ.

Prayers of the Rosary

Rosary Prayer

O God, whose only begotten Son, by His life, death, and Resurrection, has purchased for us the rewards of eternal salvation, grant, we beseech Thee, that while meditating on these mysteries of the most holy Rosary of the Blessed Virgin Mary, we may both imitate what they contain and obtain what they promise, through Christ our Lord. Amen.

7

⚜

A Scriptural Rosary for Priests

As you begin to pray the holy Rosary for priests, ask Mary to pray with you. Assume the posture of a child who needs to be led in prayer. We do not know how to pray but, as the Word of God teaches, the Holy Spirit prays within us.

Petition

Beloved Mary, you are the Mother of all priests and the Queen of the Apostles. I ardently beseech you to assist me in praying the Rosary with great reverence. Help me to be aware that I am repeating the words of the archangel Gabriel with each Hail Mary and am echoing the perfect prayer that Jesus taught with every Our Father. Ask the Holy Spirit to overshadow me with rays of divine light so that my prayers may resonate with purity of heart and selfless charity and call forth divine mercy upon priests.

Come, Holy Spirit, through the Immaculate Heart of Mary, and fill me with heavenly desire to pray for the priest most in need of prayer at this moment, wherever he may be. I do not ask for spiritual consolation for myself, but I implore that the priest for whom I offer this Rosary will receive the

*consolation of grace necessary for his situation. While I am
asking for the grace to pray well, I know the efficacy of this
Rosary does not depend upon how well I pray, but its good
effect will be realized because of Your mercy.*

*Holy Spirit, Divine Spouse of Mary Immaculate, come
with Your gifts and power to lead me in prayer. As I walk
with Mary through each mystery of the Rosary, help me to
remember the words of the patron of priests, St. John Marie
Vianney, the Curé of Ars:*

> The fingers of priest which have touched the ador-
> able Flesh of Jesus Christ, been dipped in the chal-
> ice which has held His Blood, and in the ciborium
> which has held His Body—they are precious.
>
> The priest is to you as a mother, as a nurse to a
> baby. She gives him his food; he has only to open
> his mouth. "There, my little one, eat," the mother
> says to you; "this is the Body of Jesus Christ; may it
> keep you and bring you to eternal life!" ... A child
> rushes to his mother when he sees her.... So in the
> presence of the priest your soul springs naturally
> towards him; it runs to meet him, but is held back
> by the bonds of the flesh in men who give all to
> the senses and live only for the body. As the sight
> of a spire you may say, "What is there? The Body
> of our Lord. Why is it there? Because a priest has
> been there and he said holy Mass." The priest is
> everything, after God![152]

[152] St. John Vianney, quoted in *Magnificat Year for Priests Companion*, 44.

A Scriptural Rosary for Priests

✼

First Joyful Mystery: The Annunciation

The Priest's Vocation to Holiness

Luke 1:30-32, 34-38

"And the angel said to her, 'Do not be afraid, Mary, for you have found favor with God. And behold you will conceive in your womb and bear a son, and you shall call his name Jesus. He will be great, and will be called the Son of the Most High. ...' And Mary said to the angel, 'How can this be, since I have no husband?' And the angel said to her, 'The Holy Spirit will come upon you, and the power of the Most High will overshadow you, therefore the child to be born will be called holy, the Son of God.'"

Reflection from *Pastores Dabo Vobis*, no. 20

"The Council's[153] Decree on Priestly Life and Ministry gives us a particularly rich and thought-provoking synthesis of the priest's 'spiritual life' and of the gift and duty to become 'saints.' ... But priests are bound in a special way to strive for perfection, since they are consecrated to God in a new way by their ordination. They have become living instruments of Christ the eternal priest, so that through the ages they can accomplish his wonderful work of reuniting the whole human race with heavenly power."

Petition

Eternal Father, help the priest to seriously consider the holiness to which he is called. If he is tempted to think that

---

[153] Here and in future instances, the expression *the Council* refers to the Second Vatican Council (1962-1965).

sanctity is beyond him, remind him to believe, as Mary does, that "with God nothing will be impossible." When the priest asks, "How can this be?" remind him of Your love and grace that will lead him through a life of sacrifice and perfection. In the face of his human weakness, teach him the humility of his holy Mother Mary, who relied on God's grace.

Bring him to the realization of the dignity of Holy Orders so his thirst for holiness will become real.

Help him to forsake whatever is contrary to his sanctification for love of You. Make him mindful of the undefiled High Priest, who called him to radiate the holiness of His Sacred Heart. Teach him to act, think, and judge as a priest who is chosen to serve, not to be served. Help him to see how desperately the world needs his witness of holiness.

We entrust the priest to the Immaculate Heart of Mary.

꙳

Second Joyful Mystery: The Visitation

The Priest Consecrated for Mission

Luke 1:39-45

"In those days Mary arose and went with haste into the hill country, to a city of Judah, and she entered the house of Zechariah and greeted Elizabeth. And when Elizabeth heard the greeting of Mary, the babe leaped in her womb; and Elizabeth was filled with the Holy Spirit, and she exclaimed with a loud cry, 'Blessed are you among women, and blessed is the fruit of your womb!

And why is this granted me, that the mother of my Lord should come to me? For behold, when the voice of your greeting came into my ears, the babe in my womb leaped for joy. And blessed is she who believed there would be a fulfilment of what was spoken to her from the Lord.'"

Reflection from *Pastores Dabo Vobis*, no. 24

"Consecration is for mission.... This was the case in Jesus's life. This was the case in the lives of the apostles and their successors. This was the case for the entire Church and within her for priests: All have received the Spirit as a gift and call to holiness in and through the carrying out of the mission. Therefore, an intimate bond exists between the priest's spiritual life and the exercise of his ministry, a bond which the Council expresses in this fashion: 'And so it is that they are grounded in the life of the Spirit while they exercise the ministry of the Spirit and of justice (cf. 2 Cor. 3:8-9), as long as they are docile to Christ's Spirit, who gives them life and guidance.'"

Petition

Eternal Father, kindly help the priest to understand that he is called to be Your faithful son.

May he turn to You with affection, pray with heartfelt gratitude, and trust in You. When he professes that he belongs entirely to You, let his profession of love be real.

Move the heart of the priest to self-mortification and complete abandonment to the divine will. If he becomes occupied with worldly thoughts and ambitions, let him know that he is far from You.

Help the priest to remember that he is to resemble the crucified Christ. If he cannot recognize the crucified Savior in himself, graciously bring him to repentance and conversion of heart.

Lead him to the fruitful fulfillment of his priestly mission which sanctifies him as he serves the faithful entrusted to him.

We entrust the priest to the Immaculate Heart of Mary.

❦

Third Joyful Mystery: The Birth of the Lord

The Priest, Shepherd

Luke 2:4-7

"And Joseph also went up from Galilee, from the city of Nazareth, to Judea, to the city of David, which is called Bethlehem, because he was of the house and lineage of David, to be enrolled with Mary, his betrothed, who was with child. And while they were there, the time came for her to be delivered. And she gave birth to her first-born son and wrapped him in swaddling cloths, and laid him in a manger, because there was no place for them in the inn."

Reflection from *Pastores Dabo Vobis,* no. 22

"Jesus presents himself as 'the good shepherd' (Jn. 10:11, 14), not only of Israel but of all humanity (cf. Jn. 10:16). His whole life is a continual manifestation of his 'pastoral charity,' or rather, a daily enactment of it. He feels compassion for the crowds because they were harassed and helpless, like sheep without a shepherd (cf. Mt. 9:35-36). He goes in search of the straying and scattered sheep (cf. Mt. 18:12-14) and joyfully celebrates their return. He gathers and protects them. He knows and calls each one by name (cf. Jn. 10:3). He leads them to green pastures and still waters (cf. Ps. 22-23) and spreads a table for them, nourishing them with his own life.... 'He who laid down his life for his sheep, who died for his flock, he is risen, alleluia.' The author of the first letter of Peter calls Jesus the 'chief Shepherd' (1 Pt. 5:4) because his work and mission continue in the Church through the apostles (cf. Jn. 21:15-17) and their successors (cf. 1 Pt. 5:1ff.), and through priests."

Petition

Eternal Father, often the Good Shepherd tires himself looking for the straying and scattered sheep that wander off among many dangers. He searches until He finds the miserable sinner lost in the vanity of the world. The Good Shepherd picks up the lost sheep and carries it on His shoulders, offering the greatest gift, saying, "All of your sins, your failures, ingratitude, and infidelities so numerous — I erase in the forgiveness of your sins. Justice was satisfied on the Cross, which is the bloodstained key to mercy."

Grant that the priest be a good shepherd who never tires of looking for the straying and scattered sheep! Graciously help the priest to be like Jesus, who captures sinners with a look of agape charity, a whisper of truth, and a merciful invitation to something far better, to come back to the Church's table, where the Good Shepherd feeds them His life at the altar He prepared for their salvation.

We entrust the priest to the Immaculate Heart of Mary.

⚜

Fourth Joyful Mystery:
The Presentation of the Lord

The Priest's Gift of Self

Luke 2:22-24

"And when the time came for their purification according to the law of Moses, they brought him up to Jerusalem to present him to the Lord (as it is written in the law of the Lord, 'Every male that opens the womb shall be called holy to the Lord') and to offer a sacrifice according to what is said in the law of the Lord, 'a pair of turtledoves, or two young pigeons.'"

Reflection from *Pastores Dabo Vobis,* no. 23

"The gift of self, which is the source and synthesis of pastoral charity, is directed toward the Church. This was true of Christ who 'loved the Church and gave himself up for her' (Eph. 5:25), and the same must be true for the priest. With pastoral charity,... the priest, who welcomes the call to ministry, is in a position to make this a loving choice, as a result of which the Church and souls become his first interest, and with this concrete spirituality he becomes capable of loving the universal Church and that part of it entrusted to him with the deep love of a husband for his wife.... Only by directing every moment and every one of his acts toward the fundamental choice to 'give his life for the flock' can the priest guarantee this unity which is vital and indispensable for his harmony and spiritual balance."

A Scriptural Rosary for Priests

Petition

Eternal Father, I beg You to help the priest truly believe that he possesses the celestial treasure of Christ, who loved him first. May the priest cry out, "You are my ideal, Jesus! You are not some ideal forged by human imagination; You supersede all that the human mind can comprehend. I offer the gift of myself in service of others because You shone Your divine light upon me and captured me! I donate myself to You and the Church in imitating Your life of divine love, unequaled purity, humble poverty, feverish zeal, captivating preaching, miracles, agonizing desolation, the madness of the Cross and the triumph of Your Resurrection. Only in, with, and through You can I say, 'I give my life for the flock.'"

Father, sustain the priest in grace so he will love the Church as Jesus does with the spousal love of a husband for his wife.

We entrust the priest to the Immaculate Heart of Mary.

༔

Fifth Joyful Mystery: The Finding of the Child Jesus in the Temple

The Priest, Minister of the Word

Luke 2:46-49

"After three days [Joseph and Mary] found him in the temple, sitting among the teachers, listening to them and asking them questions; and all who heard him were amazed at his understanding and his answers. And when they saw him they were astonished;

and his mother said to him, 'Son, why have you treated us so? Behold, your father and I have been looking for you anxiously.' And he said to them, 'How is it that you sought me? Did you not know that I must be in my Father's house?'"

Reflection from *Pastores Dabo Vobis*, no. 26

"The priest is first of all a minister of the word of God. For this reason, the priest himself ought first of all to develop a great personal familiarity with the word of God. Knowledge of its linguistic or exegetical aspects, though certainly necessary, is not enough. He needs to approach the word with a docile and prayerful heart so that it may deeply penetrate his thoughts and feelings and bring about a new outlook rooted in 'the mind of Christ' (1 Cor. 2:16)—such that his words, choices and attitudes may become ever more a reflection, a proclamation and a witness to the Gospel. Only if he 'abides' in the word will the priest become a perfect disciple of the Lord. Only then will he know the truth and be truly set free."

Petition

Father, You place the priest in Your house to be transformed into the living Word. You make him a minister of the Word for the Church. Help the priest to grasp the "conditions and demands, the manifestations and fruits of the intimate bond between [his] spiritual life and the exercise of his threefold ministry of word, sacrament and pastoral charity" (Pastores Dabo Vobis, no. 26).

Father, help Your priest to thirst even more for the living Word. Through the Holy Spirit, irrigate his priestly heart, which is to be poured out for his bride, the Church.

*Open the ears of the priest so that he hears Jesus saying,
"You are not alone. Abide in my word. As I extended my
arms to receive the Cross, extend your arms to receive
the Church, and remember that I am with you always."*

We entrust the priest to the Immaculate Heart of Mary.

༈

First Sorrowful Mystery:
The Agony in the Garden

Priestly Obedience

Matthew 26:36-39

"Then Jesus went with them to a place called Gethsemane, and
he said to his disciples, 'Sit here, while I go yonder and pray.' And
taking with him Peter and the two sons of Zebedee, he began to
be sorrowful and troubled. Then he said to them, 'My soul is very
sorrowful, even to death; remain here, and watch with me.' And
going a little farther he fell on his face and prayed, 'My Father,
if it be possible, let this cup pass from me; nevertheless, not as I
will, but as thou wilt.'"

Reflection from *Pastores Dabo Vobis*, no. 28

"It is in the spiritual life of the priest that obedience takes on certain special characteristics. First of all, obedience is indeed 'apostolic' in the sense that it recognizes, loves and serves the Church
in her hierarchical structure. Indeed, there can be no genuine
priestly ministry except in communion with the supreme pontiff
and the episcopal college, especially with one's own diocesan

bishop, who deserves that 'filial respect and obedience' promised during the rite of ordination. This 'submission' to those invested with the ecclesial authority is in no way a kind of humiliation. . . . Priestly obedience has a particular 'pastoral' character. It is lived in an atmosphere of constant readiness to allow oneself to be taken up, as it were 'consumed,' by the needs and demands of the flock."

Petition

Eternal Father, Your Son is the icon of obedience. Generously dispose the priest to say, "Let me glorify You with the gift of my free will." Priestly obedience invites humility and provides for the fulfillment of Your holy plan for the priest and the Church. Let nothing on earth cause him to compromise his promise of obedience, which helps him to disappear from his own sight, not having any other will but that of Jesus. If he struggles with obedience at any time, let him mystically unite himself to Jesus in the Garden of Gethsemane. Help him encounter the agonizing Jesus so that he might experience Christ's self-surrender: "Father, not as I will, but as Thou wilt." Help him to live in complete abandonment to divine providence.

Bless the obedient priest-son who prays, "May my heart be a canvas of humility, mortification, penance, self-denial, surrender, silence, and obedience according to my Heavenly Father's will, for He loves me. On my own, I will falter and be lost."

We entrust the priest to the Immaculate Heart of Mary.

༈

Second Sorrowful Mystery:
The Scourging at the Pillar

The Priest Configured to Christ

Matthew 27:24-26

"So when Pilate saw that he was gaining nothing, but rather that a riot was beginning, he took water and washed his hands before the crowd, saying, 'I am innocent of this righteous man's blood; see to it yourselves.' And all the people answered, 'His blood be on us and on our children!' Then he released for them Barabbas, and having scourged Jesus, delivered him to be crucified."

Reflection from *Pastores Dabo Vobis,* no. 21

"By virtue of this consecration brought about by the outpouring of the Spirit in the sacrament of holy orders, the spiritual life of the priest is marked, molded and characterized in the way of thinking and acting proper to Jesus Christ, head and shepherd of the Church, and which are summed up in his pastoral charity. Jesus Christ is the head of the Church his body. He is the 'head' in the new and unique sense of being a 'servant', according to his own words: 'The Son of Man came not to be served but to serve, and to give his life as a ransom for many' (Mk. 10:45). Jesus's service attains its fullest expression in his death on the cross, that is, in this total gift of self in humility and love."

Petition

Eternal Father, Your Son revealed the full expression of service in His total gift of self on the Cross. Help the priest

*to think and act like Jesus. Help him, configured to
Christ through Holy Orders, to devote himself heroically
to the service of others, bearing the weight of his cross
with the humble dignity of his Savior. Help him to see
himself through Your Fatherly eyes so he may possess a
true self-knowledge that will enable him to love and be
loved.*

*Empower the priest to discover the joy of being configured
to Christ even in the sharing of Christ's desolation during the scourging at the pillar, when He healed humanity
by His stripes. Help the priest to sacrifice his comfort but
not his honor, to live humbly in hope and never despair in
the face of unjust persecution exerted on him by a cynical
world. May the expectations of the priest conform to the
divine expectation, always simple, equitable, patient, and
charitable.*

We entrust the priest to the Immaculate Heart of Mary.

⚜

Third Sorrowful Mystery:
The Crowning with Thorns

The Priest and Confession

Matthew 27:27-30

"Then the soldiers of the governor took Jesus into the praetorium, and they gathered the whole battalion before him. And
they stripped him and put a scarlet robe upon him, and plaiting
a crown of thorns they put it on his head, and put a reed in his
right hand. And kneeling before him they mocked him saying,

'Hail, King of the Jews!' And they spat upon him, and took the reed and struck him on the head."

Reflection from *Pastores Dabo Vobis,* no. 26

"The priest's spiritual and pastoral life, like that of his brothers and sisters, lay and religious, depends, for its quality and fervor, on the frequent and conscientious personal practice of the sacrament of penance. The priest's celebration of the Eucharist and administration of the other sacraments, his pastoral zeal, his relationship with the faithful, his communion with his brother priests, his collaboration with his bishop, his life of prayer — in a word, the whole of his priestly existence, suffers an inexorable decline if by negligence or for some other reason he fails to receive the sacrament of penance at regular intervals and in a spirit of genuine faith and devotion. If a priest were no longer to go to confession or properly confess his sins, his priestly being and his priestly action would feel its effects very soon, and this would also be noticed by the community of which he was the pastor."

Petition

Eternal Father, You made a provision for sins to be forgiven when You sent Your Son to offer Himself as the Perfect Sacrifice. Encourage the priest to avail himself regularly of the sacrament of Confession as a penitent, so that he might minister the sacrament of mercy with a pure heart. Help him to realize that as he receives divine mercy in the confessional, he can more joyfully extend the same mercy to others.

Help the priest to make himself accountable to a confessor. Make the soul of the priest sensitive to sin so he will quickly seek the means of forgiveness. Aid him to be a good penitent and, in turn, a good confessor. When he is united to Christ, he will feel the weight of his sins and those of others. He will suffer as Jesus did at the hands of sinners. Provide the necessary grace so that he may respond as Jesus did—with selfless love and mercy. As Jesus was vulnerable for the forgiveness of sins, let the priest be vulnerable in the confessional so that he might become a vessel of healing mercy.

We entrust the priest to the Immaculate Heart of Mary.

⚘

Fourth Sorrowful Mystery:
Jesus Carries His Cross

The Priest's Relationship with Christ, Mediator

Matthew 27:31-32
"And when they [the Roman soldiers] had mocked him, they stripped him of the robe, and put his own clothes on him, and led him away to crucify him. As they were marching out, they came upon a man of Cyrene, Simon by name; this man they compelled to carry his cross."

Reflection from *Pastores Dabo Vobis*, no. 13
"Jesus Christ has revealed in himself the perfect and definitive features of the priesthood of the new Covenant. He did this throughout his earthly life, but especially in the central event of his passion, death and resurrection.... Jesus brought his role as mediator to complete fulfillment when he offered himself on

the cross, thereby opening to us, once and for all, access to the heavenly sanctuary, to the Father's house (cf. Heb. 9:24-28).... With the one definitive sacrifice of the cross, Jesus communicated to all his disciples the dignity and mission of the priests of the new and eternal covenant."

Petition

Eternal Father, Your Son freely carried His Cross, but He needed the help of Simon, who was compelled into service. Jesus also accepted the spiritual aid of His Mother, who accompanied Him on the way of the Cross. The Mother's heart spoke to her Son as they united in a dialogue of sorrowful love. Jesus heard His Mother: "My beloved Son, you are fulfilling Your mission. You are not alone; I am here, loving you, urging you onward in the Father's will. Fiat, my Son, bone of my bone and flesh of my flesh! Love compels you to the finish."

As the priest carries his cross daily in service to the Church, let him experience the presence of Mary and the welcomed service of the faithful chosen by You. Do not let the weight of his cross crush his spirit, even though it may break his heart. At the end of each day, when the priest is in the silence and solitude of his room, grant him peace and lead him to surrender the burdens of his ministry, laying them at the foot of the Cross.

Remind him to lean on Mary, who fortifies him with maternal solicitude. Allow the priest and his Mother Mary to have that interior dialogue of love that strengthens.

We confide the priest to the Immaculate Heart of Mary.

༈

Fifth Sorrowful Mystery:
The Crucifixion of Our Lord

The Priest's Self-Emptying

Matthew 27:33-37

"And when they came to a place called Golgotha (which means the place of the skull), they offered him wine to drink, mingled with gall; but when he tasted it, he would not drink it. And when they had crucified him, they divided his garments among them by casting lots; then they sat down and kept watch over him there. And over his head they put the charge against him, which read, 'This is Jesus the King of the Jews.'"

Reflection from *Pastores Dabo Vobis*, no. 30

"Jesus Christ, who brought his pastoral charity to perfection on the cross with a complete exterior and interior emptying of self, is both the model and source of the virtues of obedience, chastity and poverty which the priest is called to live out as an expression of his pastoral charity for his brothers and sisters. In accordance with St. Paul's words to the Christians at Philippi, the priest should have 'the mind which was in Christ Jesus,' emptying himself of his own 'self,' so as to discover, in a charity which is obedient, chaste and poor, the royal road of union with God and unity with his brother and sisters (cf. Phil. 2:5)."

Petition

Eternal Father, Your Son's self-emptying love is both inspiring and challenging to the priest. Jesus freely drank the chalice to the dregs. Christ's poverty is complete; He hides His glory and strips Himself of every possession and domain. He, the splendor of Divine Mercy, immediately forgives those who crucified Him.

The priest, aware of his weakness, may say, "I am lacking in faith, hope, and love. I am rich only in humiliation, scorn, and disdain." Or perhaps the priest is tempted to live the pride of life instead of picking up his cross daily. Perhaps he begins to chase after selfish ambitions instead of emptying himself in service to others.

Help the priest to remember that Jesus called him to intimacy, where heart meets heart. Inspire the priest to talk to Jesus about everything in his life and not to fear self-abasement.

Protect him from Satan, who strategizes to destroy his vocation completely, tempting him to the extremes of discouragement and doubt and then to pride and vanity.

Teach the priest the science of the cross and help him to understand that the cross becomes a place of exaltation because of what Jesus suffered and won.

We entrust the priest to the Immaculate Heart of Mary.

༄

First Glorious Mystery: The Resurrection

The Priest Renewed

John 20:11-16

"But Mary stood weeping outside the tomb, and as she wept she stooped to look into the tomb; and she saw two angels in white, sitting where the body of Jesus had lain, one at the head and one at the feet. They said to her, 'Woman, why are you weeping?' She said to them, 'Because they have taken away my Lord, and I do not know where they have laid him.' Saying this, she turned round and saw Jesus standing, but she did not know that it was Jesus. Jesus said to her, 'Woman, why are you weeping? Whom do you seek?' Supposing him to be the gardener, she said to him, 'Sir, if you have carried him away, tell me where you have laid him, and I will take him away.' Jesus said to her, 'Mary.' She turned and said to him in Hebrew, 'Rabboni!' (which means Teacher).

Reflection from *Pastores Dabo Vobis*, no. 33

"Renew in them the outpouring of your spirit of holiness: 'The Spirit of the Lord is upon me, because he has anointed me to preach good news to the poor' (Lk. 4:18). Even today Christ makes these words which he proclaimed in the synagogue of Nazareth echo in our priestly hearts. Indeed, our faith reveals to us the presence of the spirit of Christ at work in our being, in our acting and in our living, just as the sacrament of orders has configured, equipped and molded it. Yes, the Spirit of the Lord is the principal agent in our spiritual life."

Petition

Eternal Father, renew the priest in Your love so that he might rejoice that Jesus set him apart to proclaim the Easter miracle. If, by some fault of his own, he no longer recognizes the voice of his Teacher and Savior calling him by name, move him to shed the death wraps of sin and exchange the tomb for the light of the resurrection.

Aid the priest to hear the voice of Jesus confirming his vocation with subtle yet tangible signs. Let the priest experience the Savior's hand upon him and offer no resistance to the divine touch that beckons him to be the best version of his true self.

Father, grant the priest Your paternal blessing and affirmation so that he might experience the security that comes from knowing he is a beloved son of a Father who never turns His back. Let the Easter miracle that makes all things new be at work in the heart of the priest.

We entrust the priest to the Immaculate Heart of Mary.

჻

Second Glorious Mystery: The Ascension

The Priest's Intimacy with God

Luke 24:45-51

"Then he opened their minds to understand the scriptures, and said to them, 'Thus it is written, that the Christ should suffer and on the third day rise from the dead, and that repentance and forgiveness of sins should be preached in his name to all nations, beginning from Jerusalem. You are witnesses of these things. And behold, I send the promise of my Father upon you; but stay in the city, until you are clothed with power from on high.' Then he led them out as far as Bethany, and lifting up his hands he blessed them. While he blessed them, he parted from them and was carried up into heaven."

Praying for Priests

Reflection from *Pastores Dabo Vobis*, no. 33

"The priestly vocation is essentially a call to holiness in the form which derives from the sacrament of orders. Holiness is intimacy with God; it is the imitation of Christ, who was poor, chaste and humble; it is unreserved love for souls and a giving of oneself on their behalf and for their true good; it is love for the Church which is holy and wants us to be holy, because this is the mission that Christ entrusted to her. Each one of you should also be holy in order to help your brothers and sisters to pursue their vocation to holiness."

Petition

Eternal Father, Jesus took great care to affirm His chosen men, sending them forth with Your promise and blessing. The covenant and the blessing continue for priests, whom You call to be holy through intimacy with the Holy One. You call the priest to be a fountainhead of charity for sinners, but he cannot manufacture on his own the charity that is expected of him. First he needs to be the recipient of Your love, communicated through friendship.

Help the priest to remember that Jesus calls him "friend." Any friendship involves joys and sorrows, both of which are part of intimacy. Jesus repeats to the priest the words spoken to Peter: "Do you love me more than these?" The heart of the priest is transparent and can be filled with many loves. How is he to know authentic intimacy with Jesus? He must not pray merely in order to get through his prayers but must pray from the heart. In Your great love, lead the priest into the Sacred Heart, where intimacy is found, identity revealed, and friendship enjoyed.

We entrust the priest to the Immaculate Heart of Mary.

ↄ⁂

Third Glorious Mystery:
The Descent of the Holy Spirit at Pentecost

The Priest and Charisms

Acts 2:1-4

"When the day of Pentecost had come, they were all together in one place. And suddenly a sound came from heaven like the rush of a mighty wind, and it filled all the house where they were sitting. And there appeared to them tongues as of fire, distributed and resting on each one of them. And they were all filled with the Holy Spirit."

Reflection from *Pastores Dabo Vobis*, no. 31

"The priest's membership in a particular church and his dedication — even to the gift of his life — to the upbuilding of the Church, 'in the person' of Christ the head and shepherd, in service of the entire Christian community and in a generous and filial relationship with the bishop, must be strengthened by every charism which becomes part of his priestly life or surrounds it. For the abundance of The Spirit's gifts to be welcomed with joy and allowed to bear fruit for the glory of God and the good of the entire Church, each person is required first to have a knowledge and discernment of his or her own charisms and those of others, and always to use these charisms with Christian humility, with firm self-control and with the intention, above all else, to help build up the entire community which each particular charism is meant to serve."

Petition

Eternal Father, we pray for the priest to become attuned to the movement of the Holy Spirit within his heart and ministry. Graciously help him to develop true devotion to the Holy Spirit. May the priest experience the grace of Pentecost in a personal way and so be filled with joy!

Fill him with the mystical inebriation that comes from the indwelt Spirit. Grant that he never cease to be amazed by the dynamism of divine love working through him as a vessel of grace for others! Animate the priest's preaching with the breath of the Spirit so his listeners' hearts might be quickened with faith, hope, and love. May the anointing of the Spirit remain in him so that, like Peter at Pentecost, he can stand up to proclaim the good news of salvation with deep conviction and authority.

Help the priest to use his gifts well and to discern his charisms and those of others who are to help him in his priestly ministry.

We entrust the priest to the Immaculate Heart of Mary.

⚜

Fourth Glorious Mystery:
The Assumption of Mary into Heaven

The Priest, Mary, and Poverty

Mary's Assumption is not explicitly recorded in Scripture. However, Pope Pius XII formally defined the Dogma of the Assumption in his apostolic constitution *Munificentissimus Deus* on November 1, 1950: "The Immaculate Mother of God, the ever Virgin Mary, having completed the course of her earthly life, was assumed body and soul into heavenly glory" (no. 44).

Reflection from *Pastores Dabo Vobis,* no. 30
"In reality, only the person who contemplates and lives the mystery of God as the one and supreme good, as the true and definitive treasure, can understand and practice poverty, which is certainly not a matter of despising or rejecting material goods but of a loving and responsible use of these goods and at the same time an ability to renounce them with great interior freedom—that is, with reference to God and his plan.... Priests, following the example of Christ, who, rich though he was, became poor for love of us (cf. 2 Cor. 8:9)—should consider the poor and weakest as people entrusted in a special way to them, and they should be capable of witnessing to poverty with a simple and austere lifestyle, having learned the generous renunciation of superfluous things."

Petition

Eternal Father, You ordained that Mary would be poor until that moment when she was taken body and soul into heaven.

We pray for the priest to embrace a life of simplicity, as did Mary during her earthly sojourn. Poverty was a requirement for the disciples Christ chose, and He invited them to leave everything behind to follow Him. By Your grace, the priest can be an icon of simplicity in a world complicated by selfish greed and excessive materialism. Help the priest to become a signpost that points to the generous renunciation of superfluous things. Attune him to his personal poverty of spirit while giving him greater awareness of the needs of the poor who look to him for help. Grant him the grace of interior freedom that is safeguarded and nourished by evangelical poverty.

May the priest truly model Christ's poverty and trust that You will provide what he needs daily. Bless him in his poverty and make him rich in faith, hope, and love.

We entrust the priest to the Immaculate Heart of Mary.

⚜

Fifth Glorious Mystery:
The Coronation of Mary as Queen

The Priest, Mary, and Celibacy

Revelation 12:1
"And a great portent appeared in heaven, a woman clothed with the sun, with the moon under her feet, and on her head a crown of twelve stars."

Reflection from *Pastores Dabo Vobis*, no. 29
"The Church, as spouse of Jesus Christ, wishes to be loved by the priest in the total and exclusive manner in which Jesus Christ

her head and spouse loved her. Priestly celibacy, then, is the gift of self in and with Christ to his Church and expresses the priest's service to the Church in and with the Lord.... Celibacy, then, is to be welcomed and continually renewed with a free and loving decision as a priceless gift from God, as an incentive to pastoral charity, as a singular sharing in God's fatherhood and in the fruitfulness of the Church, as a witness to the world of the eschatological kingdom. In the world today, many people call perfect continence impossible. The more they do so, the more humbly and perseveringly priests should join with the Church in praying for the grace of fidelity. It is never denied to those who ask."

Petition

Eternal Father, we pray that Mary will accompany the priest on the road to holiness and that she, who is utterly pure with celestial innocence, will stand guard over his gift of celibacy. May the priest look to Jesus to find the meaning and value of celibacy, while beholding in his Mother Mary the perfect model of purity that elicits awe and wonder!

Help the priest to have a profound desire to enter into the rare atmosphere of perfect continence and bear much fruit in his ministry. Help the priest to recognize that celibacy does not lead him to isolation or loneliness but creates more room within him to welcome the Church's entire family. Open his heart to share in Your Fatherhood, which creates more children for the glory of the eternal Kingdom.

We entrust the priest to the Immaculate Heart of Mary.

Praying for Priests

⸝⸜

First Luminous Mystery:
The Baptism of Our Lord

The Priest Servant

Matthew 3:13-17

"Then Jesus came from Galilee on the Jordan to John, to be baptized by him. John would have prevented him, saying, 'I need to be baptized by you, and do you come to me?' But Jesus answered him, 'Let it be so now; for thus it is fitting for us to fulfil all righteousness.' Then he consented. And when Jesus was baptized, he went up immediately from the water, and behold, the heavens were opened and he saw the Spirit of God descending like a dove, and alighting on him; and lo, a voice from heaven, saying, 'This is my beloved Son, with whom I am well pleased.'"

Reflection from *Pastores Dabo Vobis,* no. 23

"Writing to the Christians of the church in Corinth, [Paul] refers to 'ourselves as your servants for Jesus's sake' (2 Cor. 4:5). Above all, this was the explicit and programmatic teaching of Jesus when he entrusted to Peter the ministry of shepherding the flock only after his threefold affirmation of love, indeed only after he had expressed a preferential love: 'He said to him the third time, "Simon, son of John, do you love me?" Peter ... said to him, "Lord, you know everything; you know that I love you." Jesus said to him, "Feed my sheep." '(Jn. 21:17)."

Petition

Eternal Father, You blessed Jesus at the moment of His baptism in the Jordan. Bless also the priest with Your fatherly affirmation, and speak to his heart the words he longs to hear: "You are my beloved son, with whom I am well pleased."

Bless him that he may understand who he is in Your sight. Help him to benefit from the continuous release of sacramental grace, especially baptismal grace, through which his innocence was restored, and the grace of Holy Orders, through which he was anointed to be an alter Christus. Grant him courage in pouring out his life and sacrificing his will for the needs of those he serves.

Help him humbly submit himself, as Jesus did when John baptized Him. May the words of Simon Peter be on his lips: "Lord, You know everything; you know that I love You." Engrave these words of Jesus on his priestly heart: "Feed my sheep." Graciously help him remember that to serve is to reign. Never let him be parted from Your love, which empowers him to be a faithful servant.

We entrust the priest to the Immaculate Heart of Mary.

⚜

Second Luminous Mystery:
Jesus's Self-Manifestation at the Wedding at Cana

The Priest as Missionary

John 2:1-10
"On the third day there was a marriage at Cana in Galilee, and the mother of Jesus was there; Jesus also was invited to the marriage,

with his disciples. When the wine failed, the mother of Jesus said to him, 'They have no wine.' And Jesus said to her, 'O woman, what have you to do with me? My hour has not yet come.' His mother said to the servants, 'Do whatever he tells you.' Now six stone jars were standing there, for the Jewish rites of purification, each holding twenty or thirty gallons. Jesus said to them, 'Fill the jars with water.' And they filled them up to the brim. He said to them, 'Now draw some out, and take it to the steward of the feast.' So they took it. When the steward of the feast tasted the water now become wine, and did not know where it came from (though the servants who had drawn the water knew), the steward of the feast called the bridegroom and said to him, 'Every man serves the good first; and when men have drunk freely, then the poor wine; but you have kept the good wine until now.'"

Reflection from *Pastores Dabo Vobis,* no. 32

"The spiritual life of the priest should be profoundly marked by a missionary zeal and dynamism. In the exercise of their ministry and the witness of their lives, priests have the duty to form the community entrusted to them as a truly missionary community. As I wrote in the encyclical *Redemptoris Missio* [no. 67], 'all priests must have the mind and heart of missionaries open to the needs of the Church and the world, with concern for those farthest away and especially for the non-Christian groups in their area. They should have at heart, in their prayers and particularly at the Eucharistic sacrifice, the concern of the whole Church for all of humanity.'"

Petition

*Eternal Father, the glorious miracle at Cana manifests
the magnanimity, obedience, and humility of Jesus, whose*

heart is always engaged in missionary zeal. Conformed to the heart of Jesus, the priest can expand his mind and heart to reach lovingly around the globe. At the altar of sacrifice, he is one with the Eternal High Priest interceding for humanity. That is the greatest miracle of all.

Help the priest to discern the gentle nudge of his Mother Mary, who will prompt him to act with the Holy Spirit. Through Mary's maternal intercession, may he become a vessel of miracles so that people will come back to the Church and believe! Make your priest a generous missionary of Your love, a new wineskin filled with the best wine to bless all of Your people with the joy of the gospel.

We entrust the priest to the Immaculate Heart of Mary.

༄

Third Luminous Mystery:
The Proclamation of the Kingdom of God

The Priest and the Proclamation of the Gospel

Mark 1:14-17

"Now after John was arrested, Jesus came into Galilee, preaching the gospel of God, and saying, 'The time is fulfilled, and the kingdom of God is at hand; repent, and believe in the gospel.' And passing along by the Sea of Galilee, he saw Simon and Andrew the brother of Simon casting a net in the sea; for they were fishermen. And Jesus said to them, 'Follow me, and I will make you become fishers of men.'"

Praying for Priests

Reflection from *Pastores Dabo Vobis*, no. 27

"For all Christians without exception, the radicalism of the Gospel represents a fundamental, undeniable demand flowing from the call of Christ to follow and imitate him by virtue of the intimate communion of life with him brought about by the Spirit (cf. Mt 8:18ff.; 10:37ff.; Mk 8:34-38; 10:17-21; Lk 9:57ff.). This same demand is made anew to priests, not only because they are 'in' the Church, but because they are 'in the forefront' of the Church inasmuch as they are configured to Christ, the head and shepherd, equipped for and committed to the ordained ministry, and inspired by pastoral charity. Within and as a manifestation of the radicalism of the Gospel one can find a blossoming of many virtues and ethical demands which are decisive for the pastoral and spiritual life of the priest, such as faith, humility in relation to the mystery of God, mercy and prudence."

Petition

Eternal Father, at the Last Supper, Your Son proclaimed: "No longer do I call you servants, for the servant does not know what his master is doing; but I have called you friends, for all that I have heard from my Father I have made known to you. You did not choose me, but I chose you and appointed you that you should go and bear fruit and that your fruit should abide; so that whatever you ask the Father in my name, he may give it to you" (John 15:15-16).

Father, if the priest is met with criticism when he proclaims the gospel, support him so that nothing will smother his zeal for the truth. Let the faithful see in their priest the harmony of what he says and lives. Transform the mind and heart of the priest so that his only proclamation is that of Jesus and the Church.

We entrust the priest to the Immaculate Heart of Mary.

༄

Fourth Luminous Mystery:
The Transfiguration of Our Lord

The Priest and Divine Love

Matthew 17:1-6

"After six days Jesus took with him Peter and James and John his [James's] brother, and led them up a high mountain apart. And he was transfigured before them, and his face shone like the sun, and his garments became as white as light. And behold, there appeared to them Moses and Elijah, talking with him. And Peter said to Jesus, 'Lord, it is well that we are here; if you wish, I will make three booths here, one for you and one for Moses and one for Elijah.' He was speaking when lo, a bright cloud overshadowed them, and a voice from the cloud said, 'This is my beloved Son, with whom I am well pleased; listen to him.' When the disciples heard this, they fell on their faces and were filled with awe."

Reflection from *Pastores Dabo Vobis*, no. 25

"The consciousness that one is a minister of Jesus Christ ... also brings with it a thankful and joyful awareness that one has received ... a treasure from Jesus Christ; the grace of having been freely chosen by the Lord to be a 'living instrument' in the work of salvation. This choice bears witness to Jesus Christ's love for the priest. This love, like other loves and yet even more so, demands a response. Jesus first asks Peter if he loves him so as to be able to entrust his flock to him. However, in reality it was Christ's own love, free and unsolicited, which gave rise to his question to Peter and to his act of entrusting 'his' sheep to Peter. Therefore, every ministerial action—while it leads to loving and serving the Church—provides an incentive to grow in ever greater love and service of Jesus Christ the head, shepherd and spouse of the Church, a love which is always a response to the free and unsolicited love of God in Christ. Growth in the love of Jesus Christ determines in turn the growth of love for the Church."

Petition

Eternal Father, we give You glory that on Mount Tabor You revealed to Peter, James, and John the truth of Your ineffable love for Jesus when You said the words that every priest longs to hear: "This is my beloved Son, with whom I am well pleased; listen to him." I beg You to allow the priest to experience Your healing Love; wrap him in the security of the Trinitarian embrace. Help the priest to respond with profound gratitude to the reality that he is Your son, chosen and loved by You.

May he be aware of the awesomeness of what is entrusted to him—the salvation of souls and the truths of the Faith. May a ray of the celestial light that Peter, James, and John saw during the Transfiguration pierce the priest, confirm his vocation, and strengthen him to be a light in the darkness.

We entrust the priest to the Immaculate Heart of Mary.

ﻭ

Fifth Luminous Mystery:
The Institution of the Holy Eucharist

The Priest and the Eucharist

Matthew 26:26-29

"Now as they were eating, Jesus took bread, and blessed, and broke it, and gave it to the disciples and said, 'Take, eat; this is my body.' And he took a cup, and when he had given thanks he gave it to them, saying, 'Drink of it, all of you; for this is my blood of the covenant, which is poured out for many for the forgiveness of sins. I tell you I shall not drink again of this fruit of the vine until that day when I drink it new with you in my Father's kingdom.'"

Reflection from *Pastores Dabo Vobis*, no. 23

"Pastoral charity, which has its specific source in the sacrament of holy orders, finds its full expression and its supreme nourishment in the Eucharist. As the Council states, 'This pastoral charity flows mainly from the Eucharistic sacrifice, which is thus the center and root of the whole priestly life. The priestly soul strives thereby to apply to itself the action which takes place on the altar of sacrifice.' Indeed, the Eucharist re-presents, makes once again present, the sacrifice of the cross, the full gift of Christ to the Church, the gift of his body given and his blood shed, as the supreme witness of the fact that he is head and shepherd, servant and spouse of the Church. Precisely because of this, the priest's pastoral charity not only flows from the Eucharist but finds in the celebration of the Eucharist its highest realization—just as

it is from the Eucharist that he receives the grace and obligation
to give his whole life a 'sacrificial' dimension."

Petition

*Almighty and eternal Father, may the priest at all times
realize that his Eucharistic mission is exalted in the heavens
and difficult on earth. For at the altar of sacrifice, he echoes
the words of Jesus at the Last Supper: "Take, eat; this is my
body." The priest experiences these words in a singular and
intimate way.*

*Help him never to pray the holy Mass superficially. Grant
the grace he needs to reconcile himself to the momentous
task of offering the holy Sacrifice of the Mass for the
salvation of the world! At the elevation of the Sacred Host,
consecrated and broken, take him into the mystery of divine
love, which captures him and obliges him to live the Paschal
Mystery. Preserve the priest from offending the Lamb who,
at the altar, becomes vulnerable in the priest's anointed
hands. May the crimson cloak of the Precious Blood be
for the priest his mystical vestment of glory and joy.
May the Eucharist be his consolation always!*

We entrust the priest to the Immaculate Heart of Mary.

8

⁂

A Scriptural Rosary for Vocations

As you offer this holy Rosary for vocations to the priesthood, I invite you to join your prayers to the following prayer of Pope Emeritus Benedict XVI:

O Father, raise up among Christians abundant and holy vocations to the priesthood, who keep the faith alive and guard the blessed memory of your Son Jesus through the preaching of the Word and the administration of the Sacraments, with which you continually renew your faithful.

Grant us holy ministers of your altar, who are careful and fervent guardians of the Eucharist, the sacrament of the supreme gift of Christ for the redemption of the world. Call ministers of your mercy, who, through the sacrament of Reconciliation, spread the joy of your forgiveness.

Grant, O Father, that the Church may welcome with joy the numerous inspirations of the Spirit of your Son and, docile to His teachings, may she care for vocations to the ministerial priesthood and to the consecrated life.

Sustain bishops, priests and deacons, consecrated men and women, and all the baptized in Christ, so that they may faithfully fulfill their mission at the service of the Gospel.

This we pray through Christ our Lord. Amen.

Mary, Queen of Apostles, pray for us.[154]

꧁

THE LUMINOUS MYSTERIES

First Luminous Mystery:
The Baptism of Our Lord

Vocations: Come and See

Matthew 3:13-17

"Then Jesus came from Galilee on the Jordan to John, to be baptized by him. John would have prevented him, saying, 'I need to be baptized by you, and do you come to me?' But Jesus answered him, 'Let it be so now; for thus it is fitting for us to fulfil all righteousness.' Then he consented. And when Jesus was baptized, he went up immediately from the water, and behold, the heavens were opened and he saw the Spirit of God descending like a dove, and alighting on him; and lo, a voice from heaven, saying, 'This is my beloved Son, with whom I am well pleased.'"

---

[154] Pope Benedict XVI, Prayer for Vocations for the 43rd World Day of Prayer for Vocations, quoted in United States Conference of Catholic Bishops, *Catholic Household Blessings and Prayers* (Washington, D.C.: United States Conference of Catholic Bishops, 2007), 385-386.

A Scriptural Rosary for Vocations

Reflection from *Pastores Dabo Vobis*, no. 34

"'Come, and see' (Jn. 1:39). This was the reply Jesus gave to the two disciples of John the Baptist who asked him where he was staying.... The Church is invited to delve more deeply into the original and personal meaning of the call to follow Christ in the priestly ministry and the unbreakable bond between divine grace and human responsibility which is contained and revealed in these two terms which we find more than once in the Gospel: Come follow me (cf. Mt. 19:21).... By the very fact that 'the lack of priests is certainly a sad thing for any Church,' pastoral work for the vocation needs especially today, to be taken up with a new vigor and more decisive commitment by all the members of the Church, in the awareness that it is not a secondary or marginal matter, or the business of one group only, as if it were but a 'part,' no matter how important, of the entire pastoral work of the Church."

Petition

Eternal Father, we implore Your paternal heart to let the floodgates of grace open for an increase of vocations to the ministerial priesthood. May couples be open to life and know the blessing of children. May Catholic families be inspired to pray together and parents be led to encourage their sons to seriously consider the priesthood. Graciously touch the hearts of young men to respond to the mysterious invitation of Jesus: "Come, follow me" (Matt. 19:21) and "Come and see" (John 1:39). By the Holy Spirit's prompting, may many men respond to Christ's unique invitation and rejoice that they have been chosen.

In Your great mercy, do not let a priestly vocation die due to human weakness or temptation from evil spirits. With paternal solicitude, help men to be courageous in committing themselves to a life that is a great gift and a glorious mystery to be cherished.

We entrust this intention to the Immaculate Heart of Mary.

⚜

Second Luminous Mystery:
Jesus's Self-Manifestation at the Wedding at Cana

The Church and the Gift of Vocations

John 2:1-10

"On the third day there was a marriage at Cana in Galilee, and the mother of Jesus was there; Jesus also was invited to the marriage, with his disciples. When the wine failed, the mother of Jesus said to him, 'They have no wine.' And Jesus said to her, 'O woman, what have you to do with me? My hour has not yet come.' His mother said to the servants, 'Do whatever he tells you.' Now six stone jars were standing there, for the Jewish rites of purification, each holding twenty or thirty gallons. Jesus said to them, 'Fill the jars with water.' And they filled them up to the brim. He said to them, 'Now draw some out, and take it to the steward of the feast.' So they took it. When the steward of the feast tasted the water now become wine, and did not know where it came from (though the servants who had drawn the water knew), the steward of the feast called the bridegroom and said to him, 'Every man serves the good first; and when men have drunk freely, then the poor wine; but you have kept the good wine until now.'"

Reflection from *Pastores Dabo Vobis*, no. 35

"Each Christian vocation comes from God and is God's gift.... It always comes about in the Church and through the Church because, as the Second Vatican Council reminds us, 'God has willed to make men holy and save them, not as individuals without any bond or link between them, but rather to make them into a people who might acknowledge him and serve him in holiness.' ... What is true of every vocation is true specifically of the priestly vocation: the latter is a call, by the sacrament of holy orders received in the Church, to place oneself at the service of the People of God with a particular belonging and configuration to Jesus Christ and with the authority of acting 'in the name and in the person' of him who is head and shepherd of the Church."

Petition

Eternal Father, You willed that Mary invoke her Son's first public miracle at Cana. Through her intercession, may many young men open themselves to Your most perfect will for their lives. Deign to bring forth more priestly vocations to address the serious and urgent needs that confront the Church and the world. The Church yearns for many more priests to receive an extraordinary outpouring of the Holy Spirit for the New Evangelization.

Open our eyes to recognize vocations that are budding in young men so that communities of faith may nurture them. Touch the hearts of young men, and enable them to go out

into the world as alteri Christi to proclaim to humanity
the truth of the gospel.

May the Mother of Jesus, full of wisdom and grace,
help raise many young men to follow in the footsteps of
her Son, Jesus, the Eternal High Priest!

We entrust all young men discerning a vocation to the
Immaculate Heart of Mary.

༄

Third Luminous Mystery:
The Proclamation of the Kingdom of God

Divine Will and Human Response

Mark 1:14-17

"Now after John was arrested, Jesus came into Galilee, preaching the gospel of God, and saying, 'The time is fulfilled, and the kingdom of God is at hand; repent, and believe in the gospel.' And passing along by the Sea of Galilee, he saw Simon and Andrew the brother of Simon casting a net in the sea; for they were fishermen. And Jesus said to them, 'Follow me, and I will make you become fishers of men.'"

Reflection from *Pastores Dabo Vobis*, no. 36

"God's free and sovereign decision to call man calls for total respect. It cannot be forced in the slightest by any human ambition, and it cannot be replaced by any human decision. Vocation is a gift of God's grace and never a human right, such that 'one can never consider priestly life as a simply human affair, nor the mission of the minister as a simply personal project.' Every claim or presumption on the part of those called is thus radically excluded (cf. Heb. 5:4 ff.). Their entire heart and spirit should be filled with an amazed and deeply felt gratitude, and unshakable trust and hope, because those who have been called know that they are rooted not in their own strength but in the unconditional faithfulness of God who calls."

Petition

Eternal Father, we pray that You protect the seminarian in Your paternal love. Graciously help him to have unshakeable trust in Your faithfulness. Aid him in surrendering himself to the all-merciful love and infinite power of the Trinity. Grant him magnanimity of heart, stamina for the mission, affinity for the interior life, adaptability to his environment, and fraternity with his fellow seminarians. In Your kindness, anoint his intellect for the rigors of academics, reveal his true identity to him, keep his intentions pure, heal any wounds that need to be cured, and equip him with charisms to glorify You and build up the Church.

When he is faced with his powerlessness, help him surrender to the power of Trinitarian love. Protect him from pride and self-reliance. Free him from himself and from disordered appetites that would hinder his total transformation in Christ.

We entrust the seminarian to the Immaculate Heart of Mary.

⚜

Fourth Luminous Mystery:
The Transfiguration of Our Lord

Pastoral Work for Promoting Vocations

Matthew 17:1-6

"After six days Jesus took with him Peter and James and John his [James's] brother, and led them up a high mountain apart. And he was transfigured before them, and his face shone like the sun, and his garments became as white as light. And behold, there appeared to them Moses and Elijah, talking with him. And Peter said to Jesus, 'Lord, it is well that we are here; if you wish, I will make three booths here, one for you and one for Moses and one for Elijah.' He was speaking when lo, a bright cloud overshadowed them, and a voice from the cloud said, 'This is my beloved Son, with whom I am well pleased; listen to him.' When the disciples heard this, they fell on their faces and were filled with awe."

Reflection from *Pastores Dabo Vobis*, no. 38

"The Church, as a priestly, prophetic and kingly people, is committed to foster and to serve the birth and maturing of priestly vocations through her prayer and sacramental life; by her proclamation of the word and by education in the faith; by her example and witness of charity.... Christian prayer, nourished by the word of God, creates an ideal environment where each individual can discover the truth of his own being and the identity of the personal and unrepeatable life project which the Father entrusts to him."

A Scriptural Rosary for Vocations

Petition

Eternal Father, You know what is best for the Church, and You do not deprive her of what she needs. Yet, while many graces fall, many seeds die because of human weakness. Awaken the faithful to pray ardently and to fast for more vocations to the priesthood. Help the faithful to heed the call to prayer even when the world tempts them not to pray. Increase our faith in the power of prayer, by which many miracles of grace occur. Set the Church ablaze with intercessory prayer for the men who have yet to discern the call to priesthood and also for seminarians, transitional deacons, and men about to be ordained. Surround and protect them with the prayers of the faithful.

We entrust them all to the Immaculate Heart of Mary.

⁂

Fifth Luminous Mystery:
The Institution of the Holy Eucharist

We Are All Responsible for Promoting Vocations

Matthew 26:26-29

"Now as they were eating, Jesus took bread, and blessed, and broke it, and gave it to the disciples and said, 'Take, eat; this is my body.' And he took a cup, and when he had given thanks he gave it to them, saying, 'Drink of it, all of you; for this is my blood of the covenant, which is poured out for many for the forgiveness of sins. I tell you I shall not drink again of this fruit of the vine until that day when I drink it new with you in my Father's kingdom.'"

Reflection from *Pastores Dabo Vobis,* no. 41

"The priestly vocation is a gift from God. It is undoubtedly a great good for the person who is its first recipient. But it is also a gift to the Church as a whole, a benefit to her life and mission. The Church, therefore, is called to safeguard this gift, to esteem it and love it. She is responsible for the birth and development of priestly vocations.... There is an urgent need, especially nowadays, for a more widespread and deeply felt conviction that all the members of the Church, without exception, have the grace and responsibility to look after vocations. The Second Vatican Council was quite explicit in this regard: 'The duty of fostering vocations falls on the whole Christian community, and they should discharge it principally by living full Christian lives.'"

Petition

Eternal Father, only the priest can say the words that Jesus said at the Last Supper — "Take, eat; this is my body" — and make Him present in the Eucharist. You bless the Church with vocations that are inspired by the example of model priests. Through the Eucharistic life of the Church, stir the heart of a future priest to fall in love with Christ in an absolute and final way. Through the Eucharist, seize the imagination of young men for Christ. Through the Eucharist, break open the heart of a man and capture him completely with Your love, which is uniquely present in the priesthood. Let love decide everything for him! Let him understand that Christ is personally calling him to the joy of becoming like his Lord in every possible way. Through the Eucharist, heal the deafness, blindness, stubbornness, selfishness, and wounds that could divert his attraction to the priesthood. Through the Eucharist, gently lead him to a future place of certitude, joy, and humility where he can say the words, "Take, eat; this is my body."

9

꙳

A Scriptural Rosary of Reparation

Every Holy Thursday, Pope John Paul II would address all priests of the universal Church by letter. In his message for March 17, 2002, he wrote the following:

> At this time, as priests we are personally and profoundly afflicted by the sins of some of our brothers who have betrayed the grace of Ordination in succumbing even to the most grievous forms of the *mysterium iniquitatis* at work in the world. Grave scandal is caused, with the result that a dark shadow of suspicion is cast over all the other fine priests who perform their ministry with honesty and integrity and often with heroic self-sacrifice. As the Church shows her concern for the victims and strives to respond in truth and justice to each of these painful situations, all of us — conscious of human weakness, but trusting in the healing power of divine grace — are called *to embrace the "mysterium Crucis"* and to commit ourselves more fully to the search for holiness. We must beg God in his Providence to prompt a whole-hearted reawakening of those ideals of total self-giving to Christ which are the very foundation of the priestly ministry. (no. 11)

The gravest sins of priests have a devastating impact, as conveyed by our Lord Jesus to Ven. Conchita:

> And the sins of scandal of my priests, what immensity they encompass! What glory they remove from me and how deep an extent they pierce My Heart!
>
> The radius those sins of scandal of my priests encompasses is incalculable for man; and only in eternity in the vision of that great light will they come to see the almost infinite evil that they produce with those innumerable sins. And I say innumerable because a sin of priestly scandal is multiplied and extends to generations.... [These hidden sins] attack the faith, blind hope and kill charity.[155]

Clearly some priests and bishops have caused grave scandal through their actions, with terrible consequences, and there is no excuse for that. We must remember that *all scandal* wounds humanity. The *Catechism* teaches the following about scandal: "Scandal is an attitude or behavior which leads another to do evil. The person who gives scandal becomes his neighbor's tempter. He damages virtue and integrity; he may even draw his brother into spiritual death" (no. 2284).

There is a need for both reparation and healing. St. James tells us: "Pray for one another, that you may be healed" (5:16). Our wounds are healed when we extend the medicine of mercy, as I found when Jesus asked me to forgive the murderers of my beloved father-in-law.

In September 2013, Timothy Cardinal Dolan gave additional insight into the *human side* of the Church:

[155] *To My Priests*, p. 20.

In her human side, the church can be imperfect, sloppy
and corrupt. We admit her flaws, but we love her all the
more because she is Christ on the cross. For most of us
Catholics, we are born into the church. Catholicism is in
our DNA, our bones, our genes. We might drift from our
spiritual family for a while, just as we do with the human
family. At times we are scandalized or confused by it. But
it is our family, our home.[156]

We can appreciate this statement of Cardinal Dolan, especially with the analogy to our human family. We understand
that most families are quite imperfect and in need of renova-
tion, but we are anchored in them. The Church is our home,
and sometimes our home becomes messy. Yet it is where we find
the Lord and His grace. Some of our greatest joys and also some
of our deepest pain occur from relationships within the Church
precisely because we are family. But our condition is worse if we
separate from family. Our weaknesses can prove to be for the
good of one another's transformation into Christ.

We can also be grateful for the various actions the Church
—particularly Pope John Paul II, Pope Benedict XVI, Pope Francis, the Congregation for the Doctrine of the Faith, and the
bishops of the United States and other countries—has taken to
correct the mistakes of the past. For example, in December 2013,
Pope Francis, building upon the progress made by his predecessor, created a commission to "look into and develop the pastoral

---

[156] Quoted by Stoyan Zaimov, "Cardinal Dolan Admits 'Sinful'
Clergy Pushing People Away from Catholic Church," *Christian
Post*, September 6, 2013, accessed November 15, 2013, http://
www.christianpost.com/news/cardinal-dolan-admits-sinful-
clergy-pushing-people-away-from-catholic-church-103942/.

care for victims and their families, spiritual assistance, mental health services, and collaboration with experts in the research and development of the prevention of abuse of minors."[157] And let us *always remember* what Pope Francis recently assured Rome's diocesan priests: "Sanctity is stronger than scandals."[158]

As you pray this Rosary of Reparation, I hope you will take comfort from these words by Sister Lucía of Fátima: "From the moment that Our Lady gave importance to the Rosary, there is no problem, material or spiritual, national or international, which cannot be solved."[159] I also invite you to ask the eternal Father to draw you, the pope, the bishops, the priests, and all the laity, especially victims of abuse, deeper into the redeeming love of the Passion of His Son, Jesus Christ. May we all be hidden in His holy wounds and pray that we can experience the healing power of divine love, for the prophet Isaiah teaches:

> Surely he has borne our griefs and carried our sorrows; yet we esteemed him stricken, smitten by God, and afflicted. But he was wounded for our transgressions, he was bruised for our iniquities; upon him was the chastisement that

[157] "Pope Francis Approves Creation of Commission for Protection of Children," Vatican Radio, December 6, 2013, http://en.radiovaticana.va/news/2013/12/06/pope_francis_approves_creation_of_commission_for_protection_of/in2-753399.

[158] Quoted by Francis Rocca, "Pope Assures Rome Priests That 'Sanctity Is Stronger Than Scandals'," Catholic News Service, September 16, 2013, accessed October 20, 2013, http://www.catholicnews.com/data/stories/cns//1303923.htm.

[159] Quoted in Stefano M. Manelli, *Devotion to Our Lady: The Marian Life as Taught by the Saints* (New Bedford, MA: Academy of the Immaculate, 2001), 141.

made us whole, and with his stripes we are healed. All we like sheep have gone astray; we have turned every one to his own way; and the LORD has laid on him the iniquity of us all. (Isa. 53:4-6)

❧

THE SORROWFUL MYSTERIES

First Sorrowful Mystery:
The Agony in the Garden

For Victims of Priest Abuse

Matthew 26:36-39

"Then Jesus went with them to a place called Gethsemane, and he said to his disciples, 'Sit here, while I go yonder and pray.' And taking with him Peter and the two sons of Zebedee, he began to be sorrowful and troubled. Then he said to them, 'My soul is very sorrowful, even to death; remain here, and watch with me.' And going a little farther he fell on his face and prayed, 'My Father, if it be possible, let this cup pass from me; nevertheless, not as I will, but as thou wilt.'"

Reflection from *Salvifici Dolores*, no. 9

"Within each form of suffering endured by man, and at the same time at the basis of the whole world of suffering, there inevitably arises *the question: why?* ... But only the suffering human being knows what he is suffering and wonders why; and he suffers in a humanly speaking still deeper way if he does not find a satisfactory answer. This is a *difficult question*, just as is a question closely akin to it, the question of evil. Why does evil exist? Why is there evil in the world? When we put the question this way, we are always, at least to a certain extent, asking a question about suffering too.... Man can put this question to God with all the emotion of his heart and with his mind full of dismay and anxiety; and God expects the question and listens to it, as we see in ... the Book of Job."

Petition

Eternal Father, Your Son was sorrowful unto death during His agony in the Garden of Gethsemane, when the sin of the world pressed upon His innocent being until His sweat became blood. He endured the terror of human suffering, the tyranny of injustice and the horror of sin to redeem sinners. He revealed His mercy by suffering His Passion.

We beg You to heal and bless the victims of priestly abuse who have shared a portion of the Passion of Jesus. You, O God, make all things new! We ask You to restore what was unjustly taken from the victims. We implore You to open the floodgates of mercy upon all victims for a renewal of their scarred memory, broken hearts, dishonored bodies, and inconsolable spirits. By Your loving grace, restore their lives.

We entrust all victims to our Sorrowful Mother, who held her suffering Son in her maternal arms and cleansed His wounds.

ᴊᵏ

Second Sorrowful Mystery:
The Scourging at the Pillar

For Priests Who Hurt Others

Matthew 27:24-26

"So when Pilate saw that he was gaining nothing, but rather that a riot was beginning, he took water and washed his hands before the crowd, saying, 'I am innocent of this righteous man's blood; see to it yourselves.' And all the people answered, 'His blood be on us and on our children!' Then he released for them Barabbas, and having scourged Jesus, delivered him to be crucified."

Reflection from *Salvifici Dolores*, nos. 12-13

"According to [the personal dimension of punishment], punishment has a meaning not only because it serves to repay the objective evil of the transgression with another evil, but first and foremost because it creates the possibility of rebuilding goodness in the subject who suffers.... Suffering must serve *for conversion*, that is, *for the rebuilding of goodness in the subject*, who can recognize the divine mercy in this call to repentance. The purpose of penance is to overcome evil, which under different forms lies dormant in man. Its purpose is also to strengthen goodness both in man himself and in his relationships with others and especially with God. But in order to perceive the true answer to the 'why' of suffering, we must look to the revelation of divine love, the ultimate source of the meaning of everything that exists. Love is also the richest source of the meaning of suffering, which always remains a mystery; we are conscious of the insufficiency and inadequacy of our explanations. Christ causes us to enter into the mystery and to discover the 'why' of suffering, as far as we are capable of grasping the sublimity of divine love."

Petition

Eternal Father, the righteous blood of Your Son was not spared. For sinners He suffered unto death. We bring before You the priests who have hurt others by some form of abuse. All have sinned and fall short of the glory of God (Rom. 3:23), but when a beloved priest falls into sin and hurts a person entrusted to him, some goodness dies within the entire Body of Christ. Although the transgressions of some priests may be horrific and people may cry out for vengeance, we entrust them to Your fatherly providence. In Your mercy, minister to wayward priests who may be suffering deeply from the interior agony caused by their sins.

We entrust fallen priests to the heart of our Sorrowful Mother.

༈

Third Sorrowful Mystery:
The Crowning with Thorns

For Falsely Accused Priests

Matthew 27:27-30

"Then the soldiers of the governor took Jesus into the praetorium, and they gathered the whole battalion before him. And they stripped him and put a scarlet robe upon him, and plaiting a crown of thorns they put it on his head, and put a reed in his right hand. And kneeling before him they mocked him saying, 'Hail, King of the Jews!' And they spat upon him, and took the reed and struck him on the head."

Reflection from *Salvifici Dolores*, no. 16

"Christ drew close above all to the world of human suffering through the fact of having taken *this suffering upon his very self*. During his public activity, he experienced not only fatigue, homelessness, misunderstanding even on the part of those closest to him, but, more than anything, he became progressively more and more isolated and encircled by hostility and the preparations for putting him to death. Christ is aware of this, and often speaks to his disciples of the sufferings and death that await him: 'Behold, we are going up to Jerusalem; and the Son of man *will be delivered* to the chief priests and the scribes, and they will condemn him to death and deliver him to the Gentiles; and they will mock him, and spit upon him, and scourge him, and kill him; and after three days he will rise.' Christ goes towards his Passion and death with full awareness of the mission that he has to fulfill precisely in this way. Precisely *by means of this suffering* he must bring it about 'that man should not perish, but have eternal life.' Precisely by means of his Cross he must strike at the roots of evil, planted in the history of man and in human souls."

Petition

Eternal Father, we bring before Your throne of mercy
the priests who have been wrongly accused and who,
although innocent, are treated like outcasts and forsaken by

many. When You look upon the priests who suffer false accusations, You see their resemblance to Jesus in His Passion. Your Son was wrongly accused and was stripped of everything until He hung naked on a cross as a victim of love.

We ask You to console with paternal solicitude those priests who have been stripped of everything and are set apart like lepers, even though they are innocent of the charges against them. In Your mercy, graciously heal any wounds stemming from the experience of unfounded accusations — especially anger, depression, anxiety, loneliness, rejection, and fear. Help those priests to learn the value of coredemptive suffering so they may unite themselves to the perfect sacrifice of Jesus, the Lamb, and let them know the consolation of Your loving presence. In Your justice, restore the good names of those who are innocent, and bring justice where it is needed.

We entrust all these priests to Mary, our Sorrowful Mother.

⚜

Fourth Sorrowful Mystery:
Jesus Carries His Cross

For Healing

Matthew 27:31-32

"And when they [the Roman soldiers] had mocked him, they stripped him of the robe, and put his own clothes on him, and led him away to crucify him. As they were marching out, they came upon a man of Cyrene, Simon by name; this man they compelled to carry his cross."

Reflection from *Salvifici Dolores*, no. 16

"Christ severely reproves Peter when the latter wants to make him abandon the thoughts of suffering and of death on the Cross. And when, during his arrest in Gethsemane, the same Peter tries to defend him with the sword, Christ says, 'Put your sword back into its place.... But how then *should the scriptures be fulfilled*, that it must be so?' And he also says, 'Shall I not drink the *cup which the Father has given me?*' This response, like others that appear in different points of the Gospel, shows how profoundly Christ was imbued by the thought that he had already expressed in the conversation with Nicodemus: 'For God so loved the world that he gave his only Son, that whoever believes in him should not perish but have eternal life.' Christ goes toward his own suffering, aware of its saving power; he goes forward in obedience to the Father, but primarily he is *united to the Father in this love* with which he has loved the world and man in the world. And for this reason St. Paul will write of Christ, 'He loved me and gave himself for me.'"

Petition

Eternal Father, as Your beloved Son carried His Cross to Calvary to be crucified at the hands of sinners, He was covered with wounds, which became the means of our healing. The Church today suffers from the wounds of many scandals. The Body of Christ experiences the weight of scandal and persecution. We have corporately sinned against the greatest commandment of divine love. The Church is in great need of the salve of divine mercy in order to be healed. *Graciously bring about a movement of medicinal reparation. Enkindle the hearts of the faithful to seek the healing balm of sacramental life. We trust that You will bring good out of the immense suffering of the Church as we humble ourselves before You. By the blood of the Lamb, cure our sin-sickness; take away our darkness, blindness, deafness, stubbornness, divisions, depression, sloth, vice, and pride. Restore our baptismal innocence that we may glorify You. Through the Eucharist, may the Divine Physician manifest His healing power!*

We entrust this petition to the heart of Mary, our Sorrowful Mother.

⚜

Fifth Sorrowful Mystery:
The Crucifixion of Our Lord

Forgiveness

Matthew 27:33-37

"And when they came to a place called Golgotha (which means the place of the skull), they offered him wine to drink, mingled with gall; but when he tasted it, he would not drink it. And when they had crucified him, they divided his garments among them by casting lots; then they sat down and kept watch over him there. And over his head they put the charge against him, which read, 'This is Jesus the King of the Jews.'"

A Scriptural Rosary of Reparation

Reflection from *Salvifici Dolores*, no. 30

"One could certainly extend the list of the forms of suffering that have encountered human sensitivity, compassion and help, or that have failed to do so. The first and second parts of Christ's words about the Final Judgment unambiguously show how essential it is, for the eternal life of every individual, to 'stop,' as the Good Samaritan did, at the suffering of one's neighbor, to have 'compassion' for that suffering, and to give some help. In the messianic program of Christ, which is at the same time the program *of the Kingdom of God*, suffering is present in the world in order to release love, in order to give birth to works of love towards neighbor, in order to transform the whole of human civilization into a 'civilization of love.' ... At one and the same time Christ has taught man *to do good by his suffering* and *to do good to those who suffer*. In this double aspect he has completely revealed the meaning of suffering."

Petition

Eternal Father, before Your Son Jesus expired on the Cross, He offered the greatest gift of divine mercy, saying, "Father, forgive them, for they know not what they do." Help the faithful to offer the generous gift of forgiveness from the heart. Aid the Church in applying the healing salve of mercy to the deep wounds inflicted by scandal and persecution. Heal the anger and frustration of Your people who are mystified by what has happened in the Church. Only by Your grace can we be reconciled to each another and forgive as Jesus does. Thank You for the many good servants who are working to heal those who suffer the scars of abuse.

Praying for Priests

We implore You, O God, to transform the wounded and healed Church into a "civilization of love." Cleanse Your house of prayer of all that is defiled and dead. Through the grace of forgiveness, make us healthy and holy.

We entrust this petition to the heart of Mary, our Sorrowful Mother.

Appendices

Appendix 1

꙳

Spiritual Exercises for the Mission

꙳

Self-Offering: Intercession for Priests

Heavenly Father, I, a poor servant, ask that I may glorify You in the offering of my daily prayers and sacrifices for the sanctification of priests. I am inspired by the glorious witness of saints who went before me on the royal road of spiritual motherhood and fatherhood.[160] I unite my offering to all the spiritual mothers and fathers of priests throughout the history of the Church. I pray that I may imitate their fidelity and fruitfulness in the handing down of the Faith to future generations.

Eternal Father, graciously keep my heart set on this foremost intention of praying and sacrificing for holy priests that they may be victorious over the world, the flesh, and the devil.

[160] In the spirit of the prophet Simeon and St. Joseph, men are encouraged to be spiritual fathers of priests also.

Praying for Priests

United with Jesus, I offer myself as an intercessor for priests in purgatory and for priests serving the Church now and in the future.

I beseech you to grant all priests and seminarians every necessary grace to persevere in their ongoing formation and interior transformation.

When the priest holds the Sacred Host in his hands at the Holy Sacrifice of the Mass, grant that he may experience the love of the Most Holy Trinity enveloping him and be strengthened.

Heavenly Father, every time I see the priest elevating Your Son Jesus in the Eucharist, I renew and ratify my self-offering for priests. It is my ardent and constant desire that You be glorified through the holiness of your priests.

I confide my self-offering prayer to You through the Immaculate Heart of Mary.

⚜

Seven Holy Communions for Priests

The offering of your Holy Communion for priests is a generous way to serve them and to grow in the grace of deepening your spiritual maternity of priests. Your time of Holy Communion is an occasion of great intimacy with Jesus. By offering that graced moment for one or more priests, you will gain much needed help for them and console the heart of Jesus.

These Communions could be offered on seven consecutive days or on seven Sundays.

Spiritual Exercises for the Mission

Seven Holy Communions for Priests

1. *Jesus, by the grace of my Holy Communion, I beg You to send anew the Holy Spirit upon all priests for their sanctification. May they be the instruments that fulfill Your prayer, "I came to cast fire upon the earth; and would that it were already kindled!" (Luke 12:49)*

✣

2. *Jesus, by the grace of my Holy Communion, I beg You to liberate priests who are suffering from any form of spiritual warfare. Send forth Your mighty word to bind and cast out any darkness that blocks their priestly fruitfulness.*

✣

3. *Jesus, by the grace of my Holy Communion, I beg You to send forth an infusion of divine love upon the priest who needs it most. All human love is imperfect, but Your love is the healing balm for aching hearts. Look with favor upon the most desolate priest in the world, and reveal Your personal love to him.*

✣

4. *Jesus, by the grace of my Holy Communion, I beg You to open the floodgates of divine mercy upon the priest who is in most need of the medicine of mercy. Graciously grant the priest the grace to accept it and become a vessel of divine mercy for others. Transform him that he might draw many souls to You through his forgiven and forgiving heart.*

༈

5. *Jesus, by the grace of my Holy Communion, I beg You to infuse new priests with confident assurance of their vocational calling. Graciously help them to navigate their mission and accept their assignments with docility and generosity. Grant them the grace of loving obedience to their pastors and bishops. Bind them to their fellow priests with cords of humility.*

༈

6. *Jesus, by the grace of my Holy Communion, I beg You to bless all clergy with many spiritual children to worship You in spirit and truth. You chose and sent them to bear much fruit as spiritual fathers. Help them tend to their flocks without counting the cost and to be good, generous fathers spreading paternal charity throughout the Church.*

༈

7. *Jesus, by the grace of my Holy Communion, I beg You to shower your saving grace upon _____ (insert the name of your pastor, parochial vicar, bishop, the Holy Father, or another priest who is on your heart). Please keep him safe in the refuge of the Immaculate Heart of Mary, who is his mother of grace. Grant him a deep and intimate prayer life to fuel all the demands of his priesthood. Please bless him with joy, peace, and generosity.*

Spiritual Exercises for the Mission

༈

Reflection: On Sanctification
(Based on the *Anima Christi* prayer)

Soul of Christ, sanctify me: remove all that is unholy in my life. Sanctify me that I may glorify You.

Body of Christ, save me: from sin, the world, the devil, and myself. I renounce sin, the allurements of the world, and the lies of the devil.

Blood of Christ, inebriate me: fill me with the sober intoxication of the Spirit. Replace my sadness with joy, my anxiety with trust, my fear with love.

Water from the side of Christ, wash me: restore my baptismal innocence. Cleanse my impurities and clothe me in the purity of holiness.

Passion of Christ, strengthen me: secure me to the cross that I might die to myself. As I embrace the cross, I renounce the flesh.

O good Jesus, hear me: and let me hear *Your* voice guiding me. Keep me in Your love that I may listen and hear Your voice as You hear me.

Within Thy wounds, hide me: graciously heal me and transform me. Keep me safe within Your holy wounds and pierced heart.

Separated from Thee let me never be: if I wander away, seek and find me, Lord. Be my Good Shepherd and keep me in the flock that You guard.

From the malignant enemy, defend me: grant me wisdom to resist evil. In Your mercy, be my shield, sword, and strong armor.

At the hour of death, call me: prepare me to encounter You in death. May Mary accompany me through the portal to eternal life.

To come to Thee, bid me: never let me be parted from You Lord. Call me to Your side; never let me go from Your embrace.

That I may praise Thee in the company of Thy saints, for all eternity: Let me see You face-to-face and glorify You forever.

Amen. I believe and I renounce my unbelief. Amen.

༈

Scriptural Examination of Conscience for Priests and Laity[161]

1. "For their sake I consecrate myself, that they also may be consecrated in truth" (John 17:19).
   Do I really take holiness seriously in my vocation?

2. "This is my body" (Matt. 26:26).
   Is the Holy Sacrifice of the Mass the center of my spiritual life?

3. "Abide in my love" (John 15:9).
   Do I enjoy being in the presence of Christ in the

---

[161] Adapted from the *Examination of Conscience for Priests* in the Congregation for the Clergy's 2012 Letter to Priests.

Blessed Sacrament, in meditation and in silent adoration? Am I faithful to making daily visits to the Blessed Sacrament? Is the tabernacle my true treasure?

4. "Come, follow me" (Matt. 19:21).
   Is the Lord Jesus Christ the true love of my life? Do I joyfully observe my commitment to chaste and/or celibate love before God?

5. "Who are you?" (John 1:19). *In my daily life, am I weak, lazy, or indolent? Do my conversations conform to a sense of the natural and supernatural that a disciple should have?*

6. "The Son of man has nowhere to lay his head" (Matt. 8:20). *Do I love Christian poverty? Does my heart belong to God? Am I spiritually detached from everything else?*

7. "Thou hast hidden these things from the wise and understanding and revealed them to babes" (Matt. 11:25). *Am I guilty of the sins of pride: unwillingness to forgive, a tendency to despondency, and so forth? Do I ask God to give me the virtue of humility?*

8. "There came out blood and water" (John 19:34). *Can I sincerely say that I love the Church? Am I willing to sacrifice for her growth?*

9. "I am the way, and the truth, and the life" (John 14:6). *Is my knowledge of the teachings of the Church as comprehensive as it should be? Do I assimilate and transmit her teachings?*

10. "Go, and do not sin again" (John 8:11). *Do I regularly go to Confession?*

11. "He ... called to him those whom he desired; and they came to him" (Mark 3:13). *Do I promote vocations to the priesthood and religious life?*

12. "I thirst" (John 19:28). *Have I prayed and generously made sacrifices for the good of the souls entrusted to my care?*

13. "Behold, your son! Behold, your mother!" (John 19:26-27). *Do I entrust myself, full of hope, to the Blessed Virgin Mary? Do I practice Marian devotion?*

༝

Litany:
Receiving and Giving Forgiveness

Forgiving others: Lord Jesus, with Your spirit of love, I now forgive and let go of any anger, bitterness, or resentment that I have toward anyone, especially toward my parents or other members of my family, including myself. Forgive the sins of my ancestors, Lord; unbind them from every form of bondage. Replace that bondage with Your healing bonds of love.

Asking others to forgive you: Jesus, through You, I ask others to forgive me for all the times I have hurt them. Bless them, Lord, and heal our hurts. Help me to correct my human weakness and enable me to understand, love, and forgive others as I accept their forgiveness.

Forgiving self: Divine Savior, help me to forgive myself, especially for those sins that caused the most hurt and that keep me in spiritual bondage. With Your forgiving love, supply what is lacking in my efforts to love and forgive others, including myself. Grant that I may receive Your forgiveness and be healed.

Lord, I also ask You to forgive me. *Forgive and heal me, Jesus.*
For the sinful and selfish use of my intellect, memory, imagination, will, and emotions, *forgive and heal me, Jesus.*
For the sinful and selfish use of my spiritual and natural gifts, talents, money, position, time, and possessions, *forgive and heal me, Jesus.*
For causing others to offend You by the bad example of my sinful behavior in what I have done or failed to do, *forgive and heal me, Jesus.*
For being resentful toward You or members of my family and relatives, living and deceased, and toward the persons who have hurt me, *forgive and heal me, Jesus.*
For all the times that I was indifferent and did not thank You or respond to the riches of Your graces that You have freely bestowed on me, *forgive and heal me, Jesus.*
For the injuries and pain that I have caused my family, relatives, and others by my selfish and sinful behavior, *forgive and heal me, Jesus.*
For the times my ancestors and I have sinned and did not remember the abundance of Your steadfast love, *forgive and heal me, Jesus.*
For being bitter and unforgiving toward my ancestors who transmitted the effects of their sins and possible involvement with the powers of darkness, which have resulted

in present disorders or wrong inclinations in me or in my family, *forgive and heal me, Jesus.*

Thank You, Lord, for Your great mercy, healing, and forgiving love.

⚜

Seven Holy Hours for Priestly Virtues

The offering of a Holy Hour for priestly virtues will draw graces upon priests and console the united hearts of Jesus and Mary. This offering can be made on seven consecutive days, seven weeks, or seven first Fridays or Saturdays.

1. For priests to be blessed by an increase of expect-ant faith, constant hope. and fullness of love.

2. For priests to be blessed and grounded in the humility of the One Eternal High Priest, who lowered Himself to become the servant of all.

3. For priests to be blessed with the graces to faithfully live out their promise of celibacy for the sake of the Kingdom, which makes them fully available to serve their Bride, the Church, with single-hearted devotion.

4. For priests to be blessed with ever-increasing sanctity to shine the light of Trinitarian holiness upon the world.

5. For priests to be blessed with zeal for God and His Church; that they may have the dynamism of the

Holy Spirit to animate their priesthood, especially their preaching.

6. For priests to be living examples of evangelical poverty and so be signposts for all members of the Church, who are called to be in the world but not of the world.

7. For priests to be endowed with the virtues of prudence, justice, and fortitude, that they might be other Christs who live His spiritual martyrdom of love, especially through the daily offering of the Holy Sacrifice of the Mass.

⚹

Spiritual Exercise on Surrender

Lord, Make Me Want

Read

"Incline my heart to thy testimonies, and not to gain" (Psalm 119:36).

"Sin is precisely this: that I do not want what God wants. And I can't see how this opposition on my part could be broken. I can't see how this prison wall which holds me captive could be pierced through.... I know precisely what I ought to do. You've often told me yourself, the priest has told me, I have told myself. This, then, is not what is lacking. The will is lacking: the being able to want. There is a will in me that wants, and there is another will in me (the same one!) that does not want. 'I do not understand what I do. For what I want to do I do not do, but

227

what I hate to do ... for I have the desire to do what is good, but I cannot carry it out.... What a wretched man I am! Who will rescue me from this body of death?' [Rom. 7:15, 18, 24] Thus it is that I am rent apart in my innermost will, and the same thing in me that wants is precisely what does not want. And this is why I cry out from the depths of my Prison of Unwilling: Make Me Want![162]

Reflect
Reflect on your interior condition. Are you a prisoner held captive to anything or anyone? Ask Jesus to come into your deepest wound and heal you by His love. Encounter Jesus in your woundedness. Ask Him to help you judge your life in a true way. Repent. Convert. Believe.

Petition
Eternal Father, I have asked that You release me from my prison of unwilling and help me desire what You want. I acknowledge my slowness in responding to Your will, my hesitancy to engage in the discipline of the spiritual life. My heart is in need of purification, of right ordering to Your holy will. I need Your help to enter into the peace and joy of surrender. I desire to glorify You by the gift of my free will. Avert my eyes from myself. I long to see Your loving paternal gaze, which reorients my vision to what is holy, good, and eternal. Heal my blindness so that I may see the needs of those around me. Lead me to renew my service to others.

---

[162] Fr. Hans Urs von Balthasar, quoted in Most Rev. Robert J. Carlson, *Jesus Christ, the Divine Physician: Pastoral Letter on Penance*, 2nd ed. (Saginaw, MI: Catholic Diocese of Saginaw, 2008), 18.

Into Your hands I place myself again. Secure me like a child in Your almighty embrace of divine love. Father, teach me how to glorify You, how to magnify Jesus, how to follow the indwelt Holy Spirit.

Under the patronage of Mary, Queen of Apostles, make me a new creation. Clothe me in new garments of virtue, anoint me, and send me forth restored by Your blessing.

⁓⋇

For Priests and Bishops:
Litany of Reparation for Offenses against the Laity

For the times I have been condescending, impatient, or disrespectful toward the laity, *Lord, forgive me and have mercy.*

For the times I was unavailable to them through my own fault, *Lord, forgive me and have mercy.*

For the times I failed to encourage and support their good intentions, *Lord, forgive me and have mercy.*

For the times I put my comfort before their needs, *Lord, forgive me and have mercy.*

For the times I withdrew or hid myself for selfish reasons, *Lord, forgive me and have mercy.*

For the times I failed to communicate well the teachings of the Church, *Lord, forgive me and have mercy.*

For the times I failed to prepare well for my ministry, *Lord, forgive me and have mercy.*

For the times I failed to counsel or listen to the laity, *Lord, forgive me and have mercy.*

For the times I participated in gossip or slander directed at the laity, *Lord, forgive me and have mercy.*

For the times I caused scandal for the laity in any manner, *Lord, forgive me and have mercy.*

For the times I failed to pray for the laity or, through my negligence, failed to aid their growth in holiness, *Lord, forgive me and have mercy.* Amen.

⚜

For Laity:
Litany of Reparation for Offenses
against the Priesthood

For the times we have not recognized or appreciated the valuable gift of the ministerial priesthood, *Lord, forgive us and have mercy.*

For the times we compete with priests, *Lord, forgive us and have mercy.*

For the times we thought our worth in the Church was compromised because of the ministerial priesthood, *Lord, forgive us and have mercy.*

For the ways we have not agreed with the teachings of the Church about priests, rebelled through our words and actions, or shown disrespect, *Lord, forgive us and have mercy.*

For the times we participated in gossip or slander directed at a priest, using our speech to tear down rather than to build up, *Lord, forgive us and have mercy.*

For allowing our anger over the abuse scandal to harden into suspicion toward all priests, *Lord, forgive us and have mercy.*

For the times we have behaved inappropriately toward priests, *Lord, forgive us and have mercy.*
For the times we neglected to pray and sacrifice for priests, *Lord, forgive us and have mercy.*
For the times we allowed our hearts to grow cold and critical and failed to treat priests with charity or gratitude, *Lord, forgive us and have mercy.*
For the times we have not forgiven priests and have withheld mercy from them, *Lord, forgive us and have mercy.*
For the times we made selfish demands on priests while failing to support them, *Lord, forgive us and have mercy.*
For the times we failed to pray for vocations or did not nurture them in our children, *Lord, forgive us and have mercy.* Amen.

A Priest Hears the Lord

During his Holy Hour, a priest began to reflect on the Stations of the Cross, relating them to his life and ministry. He invited Mary, his guardian angel, and several saints to accompany him through this spiritual exercise, during which he was seeking healing for a wound that pained him. In the depths of his priestly heart he heard the Lord:

> Peace be with you, my priest; do not be afraid. Do not continue tormenting yourself. Do not hide the pain inside yourself. With faith, pass it over to me. I search you. I know everything about you. I know that sometimes you struggle with me. I forgive you.

I know that you have negative thoughts and feelings and that you are angry with life. Please listen to me: you damage yourself if you continue this way. You are not looking or wishing for the truth of things, and therefore you remain in doubt, confusion, ignorance, lies, duplicity, hypocrisy, and incoherence. You have become so lazy that you do not have the courage to find a way out.

And going off into things of little account, you avoid the cross, which is the great and powerful solution. You will end up with depression or ridiculous pride.

Remember, I do not turn away from you. In fact, I love you still more and tell you that you are entitled to my mercy. I am not here to condemn you; in fact, remember that I did not come for the righteous but for sinners, not for the healthy but for those who are sick.

I am here in the Blessed Sacrament. Why don't you allow me to love you and act within you? I need your request, your desire, and your permission. You must ask for my help. I cannot force you! Give yourself to me with all the pain and the evil. I will set you free again. I love you, my priest.

The purpose of your uneasiness is to win you back to your right place. Go back to the peace of your first days at the altar. Remember the intense emotion of your ordination. Is anything worth more than our intimate bond of friendship? Honor me and allow me to honor you.

Remember the change in Peter. The devil has his hour, but I, Jesus, have my day. You are called to be holy in an unholy world. Take heart, my priest, "I have overcome the world." Now let my love conquer you so that you may rejoice that I have chosen you, and receive my peace.

Spiritual Exercises for the Mission

❦

Petition for a New Springtime
of Spiritual Motherhood

*Eternal Father, we ardently implore You to sound the trumpet,
proclaiming a new springtime of spiritual motherhood of
priests. We ask You to graciously make fruitful this initiative
of the Church that calls for spreading spiritual maternity of
priests, which will help bring forth an increase of vocations and
the greater sanctification of all priests. Through the heart
of Mary, send forth to all women an invitation to respond
to the cry of Christ's Bride with prayers and sacrifices for
priests, which will prepare them as agents of the New Evangelization. Through a new springtime of spiritual maternity
of priests, let the Church grow in holiness, endure persecution, and mature in virtue, divine charity, and mercy. Let
the Holy Spirit carry the cry of Christ's Bride to women in
all nations, so that together we may cry out, "Come, Lord
Jesus!" Grant that priests who are the head of the Body may
be supported by the prayers and sacrifices of many spiritual
mothers as they prepare the way of the Lord.*

❦

Reflection: Marian Consecration
and Spiritual Maternity

Marian Consecration is a covenant of love that results in the
union of our hearts with Mary's. Various saints and the tradition
of the Church tell us that this is the surest pathway to Jesus.
Our new unity with Mary draws us into her mission on earth.

What is Mary's mission? To birth Jesus on earth. God formed Mary to bring Jesus into the world, made her the Mother of the Eternal High Priest, and then made her the Mother of all priests.

While Mary's spiritual motherhood of all the faithful began at the Incarnation, it was at the foot of the Cross that her expiring Son Jesus commissioned her to behold John the Beloved as her son. Jesus made evident the primacy of Mary's maternity of priests when, with some of his last dying breaths, he labored to say from the Cross, "Behold, your son." John became the icon of Jesus for Mary, and Mary became the Mother of all priests. She would serve him as she served Jesus. John is the continuation of the mission of the Eternal High Priest. Mary beholds the beloved apostle as her own son. She gives the firstfruits of her maternal heart to John, Peter, and every priest down through the ages.

At the foot of the Cross was also Mary Magdalene. Was she not also consecrated to Jesus through Mary since she had wholeheartedly converted and was always close to the Lord and His Mother? It seems logical that Mary of Nazareth formed the holy women of the early Church to assist her in her spiritual support of priests. Women like Mary Magdalene would have been Mary's first spiritual daughters.

Now, many centuries later, there exists a spiritual army of women who place themselves at Mary's disposal. Marian Consecration has formed this army, which is also a sisterhood. Mary's daughters are her pupils in the art of spiritual maternity of priests. Humble but mighty in the Spirit, they are flower buds being cultivated in the rich soil of the Immaculate Heart of Mary. These daughters are desirous of living a life of poverty of spirit, humility, silence, prayer, mortification, and charity. They now come forth to defend the faith and uphold the priests on the front lines of a spiritual war.

Mary teaches us not only how to pray for priests but also how to serve them according to God's will. Spiritual mothers of priests carry them to the immaculate womb of Mary, where they are formed anew by the power of the Holy Spirit.

Mary teaches us how to offer humble and hidden acts of reparation and sacrifice. She positions her daughters like spiritual hedges of protection around her priest-sons. She sends her well-schooled daughters to make prayer vigils on the watchtower of the Cross. She dresses her daughters in the supple spiritual armor of her mantle of grace. This army of Marian women form a fulcrum of spiritual sanctity to help press Mary's heel onto the head of the serpent, who, above all, attacks the shepherds in order to scatter the sheep.

God ordained that Mary protect priests with her maternal grace. He also ordained that Mary have her retinue of daughters to work with her in the service of the priesthood. What are the firstfruits of being a woman consecrated to Jesus through Mary? Spiritual maternity of priests. God asks spiritual daughters of Mary to behold her priest-sons.

What is the urgency? The anguished cry of the Church is a unified, "Come, Lord Jesus!" Consecration to Mary and spiritual maternity of priests will help bring about a renewed, illuminated, humbler, stronger, poorer, yet resplendent Church at the threshold of a New Pentecost, waiting in joyful expectation for the Eucharistic reign of Jesus.

Praying for Priests

⁂

Priests Who Have Died

Reflection: The Words of Jesus to Ven. Conchita

"I do not want to exclude priests who have died. They also need prayers and suffrages so that they may return to my arms from purgatory to heaven. Even there the mission of faithful souls lasts, to free priests from that place of purification, to gain for me the joy of seeing them finally in the bosom of my glory. This will be an act of charity for them and a joy that they will give Me....

"Many of my priests, almost all of them, do not give importance to this aspect of most important charity; and they leave these intimate souls in the fire, without ever or very slightly worrying about them.

"I want that in the memento of the departed at Mass, they put their brother priests in the first place, without ever forgetting them. This is my chosen portion and the joy that I experience in receiving a priestly soul in heaven equals and even surpasses greatly the love that I professed for them on earth....

"I succeeded in saving them with my very Blood, with tears from my soul, with pleading groans to the Father, with my infinite merits; and they arise from the world contrite and pardoned. "Then, when they are in purgatory, alas! now nothing is possible for them to do, but *wait*, wait that there are charitable souls that ransom them, lessen their pain and time."[163]

---

[163] *To My Priests*, 239-240.

Petition

Most Holy Trinity, I offer my Holy Communion today for the priest in purgatory who has no one to pray for him. I beseech you to apply the unfathomable merits of the Eucharist I receive today to the priest in purgatory who is suffering the most. That I might console the Most Holy Trinity, I desire always to remember the souls in the place of purgation, most of all the souls of priests, who should never be forgotten. Finger of God, engrave on my intercessory heart this important petition, and accept my offering for love of the Eternal High Priest.

Self-Offering of Suffering for Priests

My Savior Jesus, I do not comprehend the mystery of suffering, but I believe that it has a redemptive value when it is offered in union with Your Passion. In my suffering I find solace in the crucifix, which demonstrates the selfless nature of true sacrificial love. When the weight of a cross burdens me, I desire to recall Your suffering and unite mine to Yours. I beseech You to accept the offering of all of my past, present, and future sufferings for the sanctification of priests, who are Your ministers of love. My suffering is small when compared with Your complete sacrifice of crucified love, but still I offer it to You. Please grant that through the daily offering of my suffering I can become a vessel of divine mercy for Your ministerial priesthood. These fishers of men, physicians of souls, preachers of truth, and servants of all are ministers of Your divine love and extend Your Sacred Heart throughout the Church. Please accept the offering of my suffering on their behalf so they may become increasingly holy and zealous, wise and humble, generous and pure.

Lord Jesus, draw all souls to You through Your priestly ministry, and set the world ablaze through holy priests who will do Your bidding. Lord Jesus, take my suffering into Your holy wounds, and through my offering, grant priests what they need for the greater work of saving souls.

My Savior and Eternal High Priest, may my humble offering console Your Sacred Heart.

ᴊᵉ

Reflection of St. John Paul II:
The Priest, A Life Centered on Christ

"The priest needs an interior attitude similar to that of the Apostle Paul: *"Forgetting what lies behind and straining forward to what lies ahead, I press on towards the goal"* (Phil 3:13-14). The priest is someone who, despite the passing of years, continues to radiate youthfulness, spreading it almost 'contagiously' among those he meets along the way. His secret lies in his 'passion' for Christ. As St. Paul said: *'For me, to live is Christ'* (Phil 1:21). Particularly in the context of the *new evangelization*, the people have a right to turn to priests in the hope of 'seeing' Christ in them (cf. John 12:21). The young feel the need for this especially; Christ continues to call them, to make them His friends and to challenge some to give themselves completely for the sake of the Kingdom. Vocations will certainly not be lacking if our manner of life is truly priestly, if we become more holy, more joyful, more impassioned in the exercise of our ministry. A priest 'won' by Christ (cf. Phil 3:12) more easily 'wins' others, so that they too decide to set out on the same adventure."[164]

Prayer of St. John Paul II to the Mother of Priests

O Mary, Mother of Jesus Christ and Mother of priests,
accept this title which we bestow on you to celebrate your
Motherhood and to contemplate with you the priesthood
of your Son and of your sons, O holy Mother of God.

O Mother of Christ, to the Messiah-priest you gave a body
of flesh through the anointing of the Holy Spirit for the
salvation of the poor and the contrite of heart; guard priests
in your heart and in the Church, O Mother of the Savior.

O Mother of Faith, you accompanied to the Temple
the Son of Man, the fulfillment of the promises given
to the fathers; give to the Father for his glory the
priests of your Son, O Ark of the Covenant.

O Mother of the Church, in the midst of the disciples in
the upper room you prayed to the Spirit for the new people
and their shepherds; obtain for the Order of Presbyters,
a full measure of gifts, O Queen of the Apostles.

O Mother of Jesus Christ, you were with Him at the
beginning of his life and mission, you sought the Master
among the crowd, you stood beside him when he was

[164] Pope John Paul II, *2005 Holy Thursday Letter to Priests*, emphasis added.

lifted up from the earth, consumed as the one eternal sacrifice, and you had John, your son, near at hand; accept from the beginning those who have been called, protect their growth, in their life ministry accompany your sons, O Mother of Priests. Amen.[165]

---

[165] Pope John Paul II, *Pastores Dabo Vobis*, no. 82.

Appendix 2

ॐ

Testimonies from Today: Priests

The Power and Closeness of Our Lady
Fr. Jim McCormack, M.I.C.
Priest of the Marians of the Immaculate Conception

In high school, I worked hard at my studies, and, afterward, I attended college at Yale University, where my interest in math and science propelled me toward a degree in electrical engineering. In my first three years at college, my schedule was so filled with classes, homework, and projects that I didn't have time to go to Mass. I had no objections to the teachings of the Catholic Church, and a part of me knew that I should have been attending Mass on Sundays, but my excuse was simply that I was too busy.

During my senior year of college, however, Mary began to work on me. I attended Mass at a nearby church called St. Mary's, and I was captivated by the beautiful music. A professional choir sang ancient sacred chants and motets. At times I closed my eyes and felt as if I were being lifted up into heaven.

The following year, in graduate school, I received the first indication that God was calling me to the priesthood. I was at an Opus Dei talk on celibacy. Partway through the talk, my mind began to wander. I thought to myself, "This talk is great for those who are called to the priesthood or religious life, but what about me? What am I doing here?" In that moment, I heard a little voice in the back of my mind: "Well, what about you?"

After graduating with my master's degree, I moved to Colorado and worked for Hewlett-Packard as an electrical engineer, designing microprocessors. All the while, I struggled to keep thoughts of the priesthood out of my mind. But I was only partially successful. Little reminders would interrupt my otherwise content existence, such as opening a dictionary to find the word *priest* at the top of the page, or skiing at one of my favorite resorts and seeing on the trail map a section called "Priest Creek." Each reminder would reignite an uneasy tension in the pit of my stomach. I knew I was resisting God, but still I feared to follow His call.

I continued in this tormented limbo for a couple of years. I also continued learning about and falling in love with the Catholic Faith. The more I studied the Church's teachings, the more they made sense. Beautiful sense. I became more involved in my parish; I taught Confirmation and began an adult-education initiative. Daily I attended Mass, made a Holy Hour, and prayed the Rosary and the Chaplet of Divine Mercy. My thirst to pray and to serve God and His Church grew steadily. I wanted to bring souls to Him.

On Tuesday of Holy Week of 2002, I flew from Colorado to Italy, with just my backpack, to begin a ten-day discernment pilgrimage in Italy. I spent five days in Rome and saw the Holy Father, Pope John Paul II, at about five different events. I then went to Loreto, a hilltop town near the Adriatic coast with an enormous basilica that enshrines a little one-room stone house called the Holy House of Loreto. It is believed to be the house in which the Blessed Mother lived in Nazareth when the angel

Gabriel appeared to her at the Annunciation. In the thirteenth century, the house was transported from Nazareth to Loreto in order to save it from Muslim invaders in the Holy Land. Today, pilgrims can enter and pray inside this holy house of our Lady.

When I entered, I knelt down, and began to pray the Rosary. Partway through, I suddenly experienced a profound sense of our Lady's presence, as if she were embracing me. I knew I was not alone, that I would never be alone! I could accept my vocation without fear because I now knew in the core of my being that our Lady is always there with me and will always be with me—as she is for all of us, leading us always to her Son. I returned home at the conclusion of my pilgrimage a new man and ready to go wherever she would lead me.

I eventually discovered and applied to the Marians of the Immaculate Conception and was ordained to the priesthood on July 10, 2010 at my home parish in Connecticut and celebrated my first Mass the next day at the National Shrine of the Divine Mercy, the headquarters of the Marians of the Immaculate Conception in the United States. I am so grateful to Mary for her gentle guidance and encouragement in my life and vocation. I encourage you in your prayers to entrust yourself and your every care to her, knowing that she is always there for each of us, leading us to her Son.

Praying for Priests

⚜

From Law Practice to Priesthood
Fr. Charlie Cortinovis
Priest of the Archdiocese of Washington

Every priest's vocation story is unique. Jesus and Mary have been with me throughout my whole life, but it took some time before I was open to their plans for me. I grew up in the Pittsburgh area and attended Catholic grade school, where I enjoyed serving as a lector and altar server at Mass. In college at Duquesne University, I spent three of my spring breaks in Immokalee, Florida, working with the migrant farm-worker community. These trips nurtured a desire to participate in community-service activities during my college years and beyond.

I graduated from Duquesne in 2000 and attended law school at George Washington University in Washington, D.C., where I became active with the campus Newman Center, attending daily Mass and weekly Eucharistic adoration. After my first year of law school, I went on a Marian pilgrimage to Europe, where I listened to priests speak of how our Lady had drawn them to the priesthood and how happy they were to be priests. During that pilgrimage, I felt a call to the priesthood for the first time. Yet I followed the advice of a trusted spiritual adviser, who recommended that I finish law school and work for a year to experience life as an attorney. So I continued to attend daily Mass, frequented the sacrament of Reconciliation, and made spiritual reading a priority. I also developed a greater love for our Lady, especially through the Rosary.

During law school, I began a relationship with a friend from college. She and I had much in common — our Catholic Faith, a desire for children, and many other qualities that were important to me. I tried to discern whether God was calling me to the priesthood or to married life with this wonderful woman. I thought I felt in prayer that Jesus was calling me to married life. So, in the summer of 2003, after graduating from law school and taking the bar exam, I asked the woman to marry me. Soon after our engagement, I realized that I felt no peace about this decision. She noticed my unease, and after a few months of anguished prayer and discussion, we ended our engagement. I was devastated and could not understand why God would permit a wonderful woman to come into my life precisely when I was discerning a priestly vocation. Shortly thereafter, on a retreat, Jesus made clear to me that I experienced a lack of peace about getting married because he was calling me to be a priest. My joy about a priestly calling returned, and I later explained this to my ex-fiancée. We ultimately parted on good terms because she understood that God had different plans for both of us.

By this time, I was practicing environmental law with a law firm in Washington, D.C. I enjoyed the subject matter of my work, yet I did not find it to be fulfilling. During daily Mass I was attracted to the celebration of the Eucharist and felt an increasingly strong desire to be a diocesan priest. In the summer of 2004, I applied and was accepted into the priestly formation program for the Archdiocese of Washington. I studied philosophy for one year at Immaculate Conception Seminary in New Jersey and then spent five years at the Pontifical North American College in Rome. I was ordained to the priesthood at the Basilica of the National Shrine of the Immaculate Conception in Washington, D.C., on June 20, 2009, the Memorial of the Immaculate Heart of Mary. It was the happiest day of my life. I felt strongly the presence and love of our Lady that day and have been regularly supported by her intercession as well as that of my earthly mother, Nancy. My earthly mom is one of my biggest fans, and her prayers and encouragement supported me in seminary and continue to be a source of great strength in my priestly ministry. I firmly believe that the prayers of many people, some of whom I have never met, helped me to be open to Jesus's call. Throughout my time in seminary, the prayers of many holy friends, both lay and religious, were essential to my persevering on the path to priesthood.

Each day I thank Jesus for my vocation. I regularly turn to Mary for her assistance and invite all who are considering a vocation or struggling in their vocation to turn to Mary for help on their journey. To those who pray for priestly vocations, realize how important your prayers are to men who are discerning, as I did, God's plan for their lives. I promise that your prayers will make a difference in their lives, as they have in mine.

Testimonies from Today: Priests

⚜

From Insurance Agent to God's Agent
Fr. Jeff Droessler
Priest of the Diocese of Orange

I am a priest for the Diocese of Orange, California, and have been a priest since 2009. Born and raised in Southern California, I come from a large Catholic family of eight children. My fraternal twin brother has been a priest for the Diocese of Orange since 1995.

I can say that since high school the call to priesthood was there, but other things took precedence: school, sports, girlfriends, and a job. It was not difficult to relegate the thought of becoming a priest to the back of my mind. After graduating from high school, I went away to college. While the idea of priesthood came up occasionally, I gave no serious consideration to becoming a priest.

After college, I became a State Farm Insurance agent, and through a lot of hard work and the grace of God, I built a very successful insurance agency. Although I had planned on getting married and having a family, through divine providence I never met the right woman for me to marry. I believe the reason was that the Lord knew that I would eventually respond to the call to the priesthood.

Over the years, I was able to build my insurance practice into a turnkey operation that enabled me to cut back my work schedule to approximately forty hours a week. Around the same time, I was going to Mass a couple of times a week and eventually was drawn to attend daily Mass. I was receiving much grace from the Eucharist, and my prayer life deepened.

Through the Eucharist, daily prayer, devotion to the Blessed Mother and her intercession for me, and the sacrament of Reconciliation, the call to the priesthood became much clearer, and I became open to the possibility. Eventually, I took the leap of faith and entered the seminary.

After doing my philosophy year at St. John Seminary in Southern California, the bishop asked me to go to the North American Pontifical College in Rome for my theological studies, which was a wonderful experience.

After I was ordained to the priesthood in June 2009, the bishop asked me to go back to Rome for one more year to finish an additional degree in spirituality.

If you think the Lord might be tugging at your heart regarding priesthood or religious life, I would like to offer you something. From a worldly perspective, I had the perfect lifestyle before entering the seminary: a beachfront condo, nice cars, lots of money, girlfriends, and so forth. But I have never for a minute regretted making this "career change"; I have found true happiness and abiding peace as a priest.

My love for the Lord continues to grow all the time. And the Lord has given me the grace to understand that who you are is so much more important than what you have, because who you are will last forever and what you have will fade away.

I used to insure people's cars and homes, which was a good thing, but now I help ensure the salvation of people's souls for eternity.

By the grace of God, I have completely embraced this call to priesthood and never look back. I thank God that He had patience to wait for me.

Lastly, I would be remiss if I didn't mention the role that two other people had in my spiritual journey. Although my mother passed away before I entered the seminary, I know her intercession for me on earth and in heaven have been very important in my spiritual journey. Through her persistent prayers and the example of her holy life, she greatly helped me to be open to saying yes to the Lord's call to the priesthood. Her maternal prayers are a reminder of the power of prayer and that praying for others is a wonderful way of showing love for them.

And finally, the author of this book, Kathleen Beckman, played a big role in helping me to have the courage to say yes to enter the seminary and answer the call to the priesthood through her intercessory prayers and encouragement.

(Author's Note: I will never forget the grandeur of the solemn liturgy in the nave of St. Peter's Basilica and the joy of seeing Fr. Jeff ordained a transitional deacon. He arranged for me to wear a mother's corsage since his mother had passed long before his ordination. I felt somehow united to Jeff's mother, Leona, and his heavenly Mother Mary in a bond of intercession for the birth of another priest. For that singular grace, I am forever grateful to God and Fr. Jeff.)

ॐ

The Foundation of Prayer for Priests
Pray. Serve. Renew.

Who We Are

With explicit support from the Holy See, the **Foundation of Prayer for Priests** is a Eucharistic and Marian apostolate of intercessory prayer and catechesis aimed at obtaining graces for the sanctification of priests and fostering vocations to the priesthood. Affirming the indispensability of priests standing at the forefront of the Church and following the example of the Blessed Virgin Mary, Icon of Spiritual Motherhood, we invite all Catholics to join us in this global mission of prayer and sacrifice for the New Evangelization.

Our Mission

Our mission is to advance the New Evangelization by engaging the global Catholic family in a movement of prayer for the sanctification of priests and priestly vocations through the offering of Eucharistic adoration, the Rosary, and sacrifices.

Praying for Priests

Patrons of the Foundation of Prayer for Priests

Dedicated to Mary, Star of the New Evangelization

St. Joseph	St. Catherine of Siena
St. John Vianney	St. Thérèse of Lisieux
St. John Paul II	Ven. Concepción Cabrera de Armida

Inspiration

• **St. John Paul II**: "The formation of future priests, both diocesan and religious, and lifelong assiduous care for their personal sanctification in the ministry and for the constant updating of their pastoral commitment is considered by the Church one of the most demanding and important tasks for the future of the evangelization of humanity."[166]

• **Cláudio Cardinal Hummes, former prefect of the Congregation for the Clergy**: "We intend in a very particular way to entrust all priests to Mary, the Mother of the Eternal High Priest, bringing about in the Church *a movement of prayer, placing 24 hour continuous Eucharistic adoration at the center, so that a prayer of adoration, thanksgiving, praise, petition, and reparation will be raised to God, incessantly and from every corner of the earth, with the primary intention of awakening a sufficient number of holy vocations to the priestly state and, at the same time, spiritually uniting with a certain spiritual maternity—at the level of the Mystical Body—all those who have already been called to the ministerial priesthood and are ontologically conformed to the one High and Eternal*

---

[166] *Pastores Dabo Vobis*, no. 82.

The Foundation of Prayer for Priests

priest. This movement will offer better service to Christ and his brothers—those who are at once 'inside' the Church and also 'at the forefront' of the Church, standing in Christ's stead and representing Him, as head, shepherd and spouse of the Church (cf. *Pastores Dabo Vobis* 16)."[167]

• **Fr. Raniero Cantalamessa, O.F.M. Cap., Preacher to the Papal Household**: "The Lord today is calling the faithful in ever-growing numbers to pray, to offer sacrifices, in order to have holy priests. A concern, a passion, for holy priests has spread as a sign of the times throughout today's Church. . . .

"The royal and universal priesthood of believers has found a new way of expressing itself: contributing to the sanctification of ministerial priesthood. Such vocations are extending out more and more beyond the walls of the cloistered monasteries, where they have been hidden, and are reaching the faithful. This vocation is becoming widespread, a call that God addresses to many."[168]

History

In 2007, the Vatican's Congregation for the Clergy issued a booklet to bishops all over the world titled *Eucharistic Adoration for the Sanctification of Priests and Spiritual Maternity.* With the release of the booklet, a movement of prayer was initiated but not formalized.

[167] Quoted in *Eucharistic Adoration for the Sanctification of Priests and Spiritual Maternity* (2012 edition), pp. 8-9.
[168] Raniero Cantalamessa, O.F.M. Cap., *Sober Intoxication of the Spirit, Part Two: Born Again of Water and the Spirit* (Cincinnati: Servant Books, 2012), 60.

Praying for Priests

The inspiration for the founding of the **Foundation of Prayer for Priests** began on pilgrimage to the Holy Land in 2013, when a priest working in Rome presented Kathleen Beckman with the Congregation's second edition of *Eucharistic Adoration for the Sanctification of Priests and Spiritual Maternity*. After receiving inspiration at the Rock of Calvary in the Church of the Holy Sepulchre, Kathleen wrote a letter to the Congregation, proposing to enlist a team of priests and laity to create an apostolate to promote the Congregation's blueprint of *Eucharistic Adoration for the Sanctification of Priests and Spiritual Maternity*. Kathleen received a written response in May of 2013 with a protocol number from Mauro Cardinal Piacenza, then prefect of the Congregation for the Clergy. In the name of the Congregation, Cardinal Piacenza graciously conveyed not only his approval but also his encouragement. A founding team of priests and laity with episcopal advisers has been formed.

Coinciding with the launch of the **Foundation of Prayer for Priests** is the debut of the website www.foundationforpriests.org and the release of the book *Praying for Priests: A Mission for the New Evangelization* by Kathleen Beckman.

Membership: Join the Mission!

Pray. Offer prayers and sacrifices in communion with the Congregation for the Clergy for the personal holiness of all priests and for vocations to the priesthood, in one or more of the following ways:

- Spiritual adoption of a priest or seminarian
- Eucharistic adoration (individual or communal)
- The holy Rosary

- Vianney cenacles (prayer groups affiliated with FPP) in homes, parishes, and organizations

- Family prayer

- Fasting

- The offering of personal suffering for the sanctification of priests

- Registration of your spiritual endowments for priests and seminarians at www.foundationforpriests.org. The apostolate will report your spiritual offerings to the Congregation for the Clergy. You can invite others to do the same.

Serve. Support the ministerial priesthood for the advancement of the New Evangelization with your time, talents, and resources:

- Visit www.foundationforpriests.org to learn about ways to promote intercessory prayer for priests in your parish or diocese, especially through Eucharistic adoration and prayer cenacles.

- Learn how to work with bishops and priests in the promotion of vocations and spiritual maternity/paternity of priests as ways to advance the New Evangelization.

- Learn to serve as Mary serves: humbly, obediently, generously, faithfully, selflessly, and with eyes always fixed on the Eternal High Priest.

Renew. Intercessory prayer and sacrifice are more important than ever for the interior renewal of priests, who are at the forefront of the New Evangelization. You can be a vital part of this renewal by learning about and incorporating the following into your spiritual life:

Praying for Priests

- The necessity of holy priests and priestly vocations
- The priority of intercessory prayer and sacrifice for priests
- The fruitfulness of Eucharistic life
- The beauty and importance of Marian spirituality
- The blessings of spiritual maternity and paternity
- The universal call to holiness
- How to live spiritual lives as contemplatives in action

All are invited to become members of the **Foundation of Prayer for Priests** and join the Church's crusade of intercession for the sanctification of priests and vocations.

For more information on how to impact the lives of priests throughout the world, please visit www.foundationforpriests.org or contact us at info@foundationforpriests.org.

⁂

About the Author

Kathleen Beckman, L.H.S., is an author, Catholic radio host, retreat director, and Co-founder and President of the Foundation of Prayer for Priests. She is a popular speaker at seminaries, convents, conferences, and parishes in the United States and abroad. She has been featured on EWTN Television and Radio, and her writings have been published in *Magnificat* magazine and on *Catholic Exchange*.

Kathleen hosts the weekly program *Living Eucharist*, which airs internationally on Radio Maria and features interviews with bishops, priests, seminarians, religious, and lay leaders on a variety of spiritual topics.

Kathleen speaks and writes about Eucharistic life, prayer, sacramental healing and deliverance, Mary, the vocation of women, co-redemptive suffering, chastity, divine mercy, family, spiritual motherhood of priests, the interior renewal of priests, and the New Evangelization.

Her previous books include *Rekindle Eucharistic Amazement*, *Behold the Lamb of God*, and *The Holy Rosary for Purity*.

Since 1991, Kathleen has served in leadership for Magnificat, A Ministry to Catholic Women, an international apostolate. In 2002, she was invested as a Lady of the Equestrian Order of the

Holy Sepulchre of Jerusalem. Since 2002, she has worked with priests in the ministry of healing and deliverance, and in 2013, she became a faculty member and spiritual director at the Pope Leo XIII Institute.

Also a small business owner, Kathleen previously worked in the field of medical assistance and administration. She is married with two sons and lives in Orange, California.

Learn more at www.kathleenbeckman.com.